# IMAGES & ICONS
## OF THE
# NEW WORLD

## ESSAYS ON AMERICAN CARTOGRAPHY

*Edited by*
*Karen Severud Cook*

THE BRITISH LIBRARY

FIRST PUBLISHED IN *THE BRITISH LIBRARY JOURNAL*, XXII/1, SPRING 1996

© 1996 THE BRITISH LIBRARY BOARD

ISBN 0 7123 4520 5  1001402131

COVER DESIGNED BY JOHN MITCHELL

PRINTED IN GREAT BRITAIN BY
THE UNIVERSITY PRESS, CAMBRIDGE

# IMAGES & ICONS
## OF THE
# NEW WORLD

# CONTENTS

IN

MEMORY

OF

# HELEN WALLIS, O.B.E.

## 1924–1995

MAP LIBRARIAN

OF

THE BRITISH LIBRARY

The colour plates in these essays are the generous gift of
*The Friends of the British Library*
who benefited greatly from the support of
Helen Wallis
over many years

# 'A VERY COMMON AND USUALL TRADE': THE RELATIONSHIP BETWEEN CARTOGRAPHIC PERCEPTIONS AND 'FISHING' IN THE DAVIS STRAIT *CIRCA* 1500–1550

KIRSTEN A. SEAVER

FROM the time it was certain that one could sail westwards from Europe and reach land on the other side of the ocean, three kinds of European travellers headed west into the northern Atlantic: those searching for a north-west passage to the spices and silks of the Orient through what soon became known as an intervening American continent; those hoping to find gold or silver ashore in the New World; and those content to exploit everyday commodities obtainable from the eastern shore of North America and its adjacent waters.

The discussion below will examine indications that, in the first half of the sixteenth century, at least some cartographers of the New World bordering the North Atlantic (fig. 1) tempered their work with knowledge obtained through a slow but steady trickle of information from returning fishermen, a comprehensive vocation, as will become evident.

## NORTH ATLANTIC FISHERIES IN MAPS AND DOCUMENTS

The period *circa* 1500–1550 is challenging to research because documentary material is especially scarce, but the maps themselves contain clues to their origins. It is true that in 1558 Nicolò Zeno confused northern cartography and exploration for generations to come with the publication in Venice of his map of the northern Atlantic, supposedly based on voyages made in the 1380s by his ancestors. However, despite the Zeno map's non-existent lands and islands, the innumerable named locations in Iceland and such easily recognizable seamarks as 'Scusenes' (Skudenes) southwest of Bergen in Norway and 'S. Magnus' (St Magnus Cathedral in Kirkwall) in the Orkneys indicate that this map had its roots in the northern codfish trade. Even firmer evidence is provided by the printed world map completed by Johann Ruysch in 1507 and published in the 1508 Rome edition of Ptolemy's *Geographia*.

Ruysch's map (fig. 2) bears out the truth of Marcus Beneventanus's statement in the

I

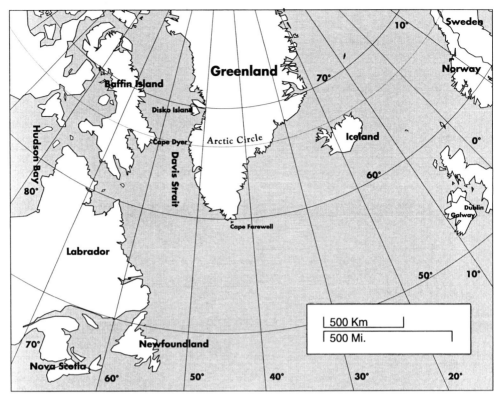

*Fig. 1.* Modern delineation of the North Atlantic region. By David Olaf Seaver

introduction ('Orbis nova descriptio') to the 1508 volume that Ruysch had himself gone on a voyage to the new lands in the west, sailing from the south of England along the fifty-third parallel before heading somewhat northwards. At the time Ruysch was most likely to have made this voyage, around 1502–4, Bristol fishermen and codfish merchants were already exploiting the New World fishing banks on a large scale.[1] Any number of Bristol veterans in the codfish business could have told Ruysch that Vardø in distant north-eastern Norway had a church named St Olaf's ('Sāct. Odulfi' on the Ruysch map and 'S. Olavi' on the 1539 *Carta marina* by Olaus Magnus); Vardø was so central to the international codfish trade as a fishing port and to the Norwegian archbishop's income that Archbishop Jørund himself had gone to Finnmark to consecrate the first church there in 1307.[2] And the same group of Bristol men would have been as well informed about the shape of southern Greenland as about the route thither.

Such knowledge is much more clearly apparent on Ruysch's map than on his Portuguese and Italian map sources, which showed Greenland as the westernmost point of a Eurasian continent on maps derived from the *circa* 1427 work of the Danish

2

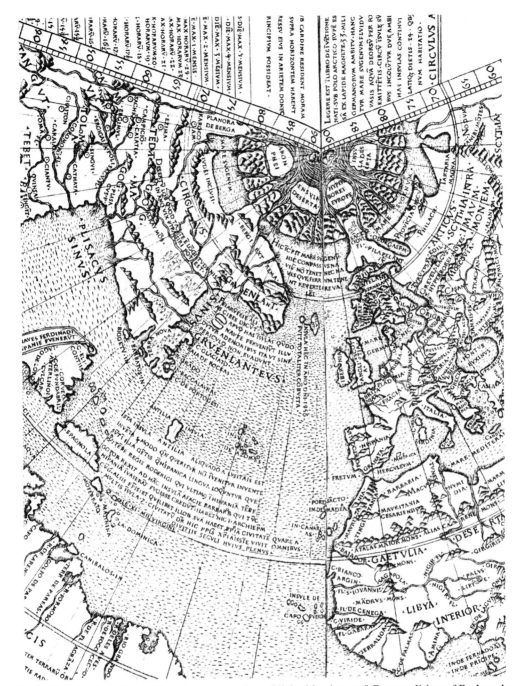

*Fig. 2.* Detail of world map by Johann Ruysch, published in the 1508 Rome edition of Ptolemy's *Geographia*. This is the version reproduced by A. E. Nordenskiöld in his 1889 facsimile atlas (see pl. xxxii and text), which calls the Davis Strait the 'Bay of Greenland'. The Ruysch map in the two original copies of the Rome Ptolemy in the British Library Map Library (Maps C.1.d.5 and Maps C.1.d.6) does not have this place name. BL, Maps 5.e.9

3

cartographer Claudius Clavus, or as a disembodied promontory reaching down from the North as in the 1502 Cantino map (Plate I). Ruysch showed Greenland as the huge, northeastern promontory of the American continental land mass, separated from Europe by a wide body of water. Mariners sailing to Greenland from the western British Isles would have perceived Greenland's relative location just as Ruysch depicted it, and they would have been aware of Greenland's overwhelming proportions, even if they had no more idea than anyone else that the country was an island.

On Ruysch's map a wide bay separates the large 'Grvenlant' promontory from the area called 'Terra Nova'. This bay, which obviously represents the lower and most navigable part of the Davis Strait, is called 'Sinvs Grvenlantevs' (the Bay of Greenland) on the Ruysch map which A. E. Nordenskiöld reproduced in his *Facsimile Atlas* from his own copy of the 1508 Rome Ptolemy, but the bay is unnamed on the Ruysch maps in the British Library's two originals of the 1508 *Geographia*.[3] We do not know what made Ruysch add to or subtract from his plates a name suggesting that his English informants were accustomed to sailing *from* a known Greenland *to* an imperfectly known 'Terra Nova', or why he and others did not build upon his performance later.[4] Many subsequent maps depict the Davis Strait as a bay, however, and suggest that the mapmakers directly or indirectly drew on information from voyagers who had continued north into the Davis Strait until stopped by pack ice spanning the Davis Strait and making Greenland and Canada appear as a U-shaped coastline bordered to the north by polar wastes. Like the delineations on the maps themselves, voyagers' perceptions of the latitude at which the 'bay' became impenetrable would have varied greatly, not only with the particular year and season, but also with their reasons for heading north along the Labrador and Greenland coasts.

There must have been many more such voyagers than appear in written records. While exploration ventures and the pursuit of precious metals or other luxury goods were visible and glamorous, farming, hunting, logging, and fishing were not. Successful voyages of discovery produced fame and recorded licences as well as a wealth of information about new territories and sailing routes which found its way into cartography, but the historical value of these early accounts and maps should not blind us to their shortcomings. Explorers' reports were intended to impress past and future sponsors, and the information they contained reflected specific voyages undertaken at one particular time of year. On maps cartographers sometimes superimposed their cosmographical theories as idiosyncratically as the famous navigators of the day told their tales. In addition, the maps most likely to reflect new information accurately were often the most closely guarded for reasons of national interest.

We must also take into consideration the far-reaching effects of the 1494 Treaty of Tordesillas, which decreed that all newly discovered land east of a line drawn about 960 nautical miles west of the Cape Verde Islands belonged to Portugal, while everything to the west of it was Spanish territory. The restrictions imposed by this treaty made the eastward-tending coast of North America an especially tempting target for loosely defined delineations from which the Portuguese stood most to gain. This inexactness was

4

exacerbated by the lack of adequate instruments for determining longitude (east–west distance) accurately and by the phenomenon of compass deviation, which made true north almost impossible to assess. Sixteenth-century European navigators knew that compass deviation was a problem, but they were a long way from understanding its variable nature.

Fishermen and traders whose business took them to distant places knew from accumulated and repeated experience what to expect along their route and at their destination. Many fifteenth- and sixteenth-century explorers must have been made party to such knowledge during their early sailing days, even if they did not write the information down or credit their later feats to a basic training their colleagues would have taken for granted. Although every bit as dangerous as any voyage of exploration, fishing was and is an unglamorous business producing commonly available foods. It clearly held little appeal for fifteenth- and sixteenth-century chroniclers of North Atlantic and North American exploration.

Fishing and related activities had such a low profile that, were it not for their enduring economic importance to every country on Europe's Atlantic seaboard, even the patchy documentation of rapidly burgeoning activities along the facing American shores, from present-day New England northwards, would not exist. Historians owe much to the Portuguese King's imposition of duty on Newfoundland cod in 1506 and to the litigious Hugh Elyot of Bristol, whose Newfoundland ventures (at least in part on the strength of the royal licence young Sebastian Cabot had inherited from his father) appear to have ended on a sour note in 1505 when he sued his Portuguese collaborator, Francisco Fernandes, for money owed.[5] The sparse records about northern venturers – Iberian as well as English – caused López de Gómara to lament in 1553 that 'there is no recollection left by any of them so far as I know, particularly those who steered northward, coasting the Bacallaos region and Labrador'.[6] Although the early and widespread use of the name 'Bacallaos' (codfish) to indicate Newfoundland and its adjacent areas bears clear testimony to the importance of the fishing industry, as growing populations everywhere increased the need for cheap protein, it is easy to find examples of indifference to the fishing business among educated people in England and elsewhere.

John Dee (1527–1608), who had opinions on almost every subject from the Queen's horoscope to matters of exploration and cartography, mistakenly thought that Nicholas of Lynn was the author of *Inventio Fortunata* describing a voyage to Greenland and into the Davis Strait in the year 1360. It was a voyage of exploration believed to have produced valuable information about the polar regions, but in and of itself Dee found this northern voyage by an Englishman unexceptional. He noted that from Lynn to Iceland 'it is not above a fortnights sayling with an ordinary winde, and hath beene of many yeeres a very common and usuall trade...'.[7]

Hugh Willoughby, whose voyage of 1553–4 in search of a north-east passage to Cathay ended in disaster, fully shared Dee's dismissive attitude towards the northern codfish trade. Upon reaching the island of 'Seynam' (Senja) in north-western Norway, he wrote that 'there was no merchandize there, but onely dryed fish, and traine oyle [from fish livers]'.[8] We find an equally lofty disdain in Diogo Ribeiro's two maps from 1529, on which he noted that there was 'nothing of value' to be found in the 'Tiera del Labrador', a region he said was discovered by the English (and which may well have included Greenland).[9] On one of those 1529 maps he added that these Englishmen were from Bristol.[10] Just two years earlier, the Bristolian Robert Thorne the Younger had sent a map of his own making (fig. 3) to the English Ambassador in Seville (where the Portuguese-born Ribeiro had succeeded Sebastian Cabot as Pilot Major) together with a letter claiming that his father and Hugh Elyot had discovered North America before Sebastian's father, John Cabot, arrived in the New World.[11] It is tempting to interpret Ribeiro's 1529 message as: 'Keep the useless place'.

The Thornes were part of the same inner circle of wealthy Bristol traders in codfish and other goods who gathered around John and Sebastian Cabot by turn. But although John Cabot enjoyed being celebrated in Bristol and London for the success of his 1497 voyage to 'Asia' (North America), he had not reached his own goal of finding a north-west route to Cathay, so it was of little interest to him that the Newfoundland waters were thick with codfish, as his Bristol crew had reported in London.[12] The following year he set off on his ill-fated last quest, leaving behind in Bristol his ambitious young son Sebastian. Other Bristol merchants were also eager to profit from easier access to the silks and spices of the Orient should the opportunity arise, but they meanwhile made do with fish and other daily necessaries, such as leather and cloth, drawing upon their long experience in trading through a network spanning the whole known western world.

Bristol men also had long practice in hauling up their own fish from distant fishing banks. The Anglo-Icelandic 'cod wars' began in the early fifteenth century, and it is likely that two much-discussed expeditions which left Bristol for the 'Isle of Brazil' in 1480 and 1481 constituted the first English attempts to sail directly *to* the Newfoundland-Labrador region, after some decades of following roughly the fifty-third parallel when returning home from exploiting the rich North American fishing banks via a triangular course which included Greenland. Their first contact with the American coast, after crossing the narrowing Davis Strait with the current from Greenland, would have been the upper Labrador coast, an important point to keep in mind when studying both Thorne's map (fig. 3) and Sebastian Cabot's printed map (fig. 4) from 1544.[13]

NORTH ATLANTIC FISHERIES AS SOURCES OF 'SEA MONSTERS'
DEPICTED ON MAPS

Before asking how much Sebastian Cabot's early knowledge of New World fishing routes may have influenced his quests for the north-west passage to Cathay, and before comparing his one surviving work with a couple of other maps from the first half of the sixteenth century which appear to show the Davis Strait in some form, we must make a detour into sixteenth-century taxonomy to see what 'fish' meant to people at that time, and why 'fishing' may have caused people to sail even farther north into the Davis Strait than a quest for cod and halibut would seem to warrant. Contemporary ideas of marine

*Fig. 3.* Detail of map drawn by Robert Thorne the Younger in 1527. From Richard Hakluyt, *The Principal Navigations ... of the English Nation* (Glasgow, 1903), vol. ii, pp. 159–81 (the map is between pp. 176–7). BL, 10024.k.3

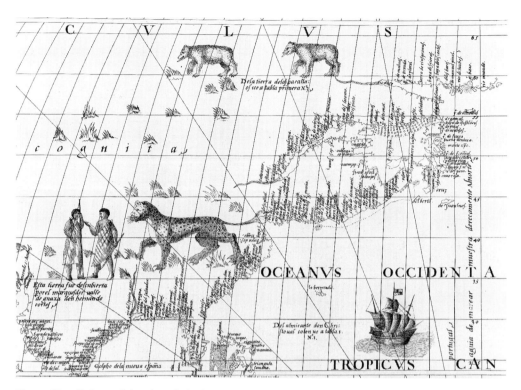

*Fig. 4.* Detail from Sebastian Cabot's 1544 map, now in the Bibliothèque Nationale in Paris. Reproduced here from M. Jomard, *Les Monuments de la géographie* (Paris), pl. xx.1. BL, Maps Ref. A.6(1)

creatures were as confused as the cartography and geographical writing about the far northern regions and depended on the same disparate, but interconnected, sources of information.

Konrad Gesner's mid-sixteenth-century illustrated compendium on fishes shows that educated Europeans knew about a great variety of creatures in the sea, creatures we would still recognize as fish today as well as some that never existed.[14] Spiked and scaly monsters abound on his pages as they do in reality. Many sea mammals were also counted as fish, for example 'whalefish'. Selma Barkham's studies of early Basque whaling in Newfoundland show how the New World whale fishery began as an outgrowth of codfishing expeditions in 'Terranova', a non-specific name referring to the entire coast and all the islands belonging to Canada and the northeasternmost part of the United States. The enterprising Englishman Thomas Buxer had both fish and whale in the cargo he brought straight from Iceland to Spain in 1498.[15] A linguistic distinction in casual notices about fishing vessels or fishermen was not likely for as long as fishing and whaling were considered part of the same 'common and usuall trade'.

8

An entry in the *Chronicles of London* for 1456 suggests that the English of that time distinguished 'iiij great ffyshes, wherof one was callid mors maryne, and the second a swerdfysshe, and the other ij were whalis', caught in the Thames estuary. To Gesner and his learned continental contemporaries even a hundred years later, however, the supposed male of one species of 'whalefish' had tusks and thick, bristly whiskers and was called, among other things, a 'morse' (the Latin word *morsus* means a bite or biting – something involving formidable teeth), a 'Russor' or a 'Rostinger'. Known to us as *Odobenus rosmarus rosmarus*, the Atlantic walrus appears in fig. 5 as depicted in Gesner's book, where he also shows it as a 'Rosmaro' from Olaus Magnus's *Carta marina* of 1539.[16]

Gesner (who also refers to the walrus as a 'sea elephant' and a 'Russian whale') notes that according to Olaus Magnus, the 'Russor' is the size of a whale, but adds that this could not be proved by the specimen exhibited at the end of 1519 in the town hall of Strasbourg in Alsace, together with the drawing in fig. 5 and a doggerel poem in German, both intended to convey factual knowledge about the display. The centrepiece of the travelling exhibition was a young and small 'Russor' killed and shipped 'from Scandinavia' in 1519, whose head had been cut off and sent to Pope Leo X in a barrel of salt. The unknown Vatican artist who drew the salted head of the so-called *Cetus dentatus* ('toothed whale') in fig. 5 must have added the body from a verbal description. According to the poem, the creature had a female counterpart known as the *Balena* or baleen whale.[17]

To an inland audience, the 'Russor' by any name must have seemed an exotic creature indeed, and we cannot wonder if news of its presence in the neighbourhood stirred the imagination of Albrecht Dürer of Nuremberg, whose exquisite studies of humans and animals show him to have been a keen observer of nature, and whose connection with German cartographic publishing reveals his wish to take an active part in the dissemination of new knowledge. Gesner's information that 'Alberto' (Albrecht Dürer) had also described the 'Russor' does not refer directly to Dürer's exquisite coloured wash drawing (fig. 6), now in the British Museum, of a walrus head in the same bedraggled condition as the one seen by the Vatican artist.[18] But there is good reason to believe that the same model served for both pictures. Dürer took down no more and no less than what he saw whenever he drew from life; it would have been in keeping with his usual practice if, confronted with the salted head, he refused to attach an imagined body to his portrait of the head, preferring to add his own description later of this animal whose name he seems not to have known, and about which learned men could have taught him little.

It is unlikely that those who hunted walrus in the first half of the sixteenth century worried about the nomenclature and zoological distinctions of sea mammals, but Dutch fishermen to whom Dürer evidently showed his drawing on a visit to Zeeland in December 1520, occasioned by his wish to see another sea monster (a huge whale reportedly stranded there), clearly had no trouble recognizing the creature in his picture. Above his signature and below the date '1521' Dürer added this terse description: 'The

9

Rusor in Norweg nenpet man micht
C ais deuit as bin doch ich
Mein Weib / † balena ist genannt
Im Oceantischen Meer bekannt :
Mache vngewitter groß im Meer
Schreckt Altrantrum vnd sein Heer.
Dem Solten Meer dem streich ich nach/
Zu streit vnd fechten ist mir gach
Man findt viel tau end mein genossen/
Die lang Zän hand auß der massen
Die sind 2. 3. 4. elen lang/
Vnd so dick wie ein Zilgstang.
Daist ein fechten vnd ein reissen/
Mit den Wallfischen wir vns beissen.
Vnd all Fisch die wir kummen an/
Die mögen für vns nicht bestan.
Doch hand mich etlich so getrieben/
Daß ich im Meer nicht bin geblieben/
Sondern must weichen an den staden/
Da nam ich mein tödtlichen schaden.
Zwentzig acht schuch maß mich aus mas/
Wiewol ein klein Rusor ich war.
Solt ich mein zeit sollen leben/
Ich hett nichts vmb all Wallfisch geben.
Den Nidressa der Bischoff hat/
Mich stechen lassen an ein gstad.
Bapst Leo meinen Kopff gesehen eht.
Gen Rom da mich mänch Mensch anblickt.
Zu Straßburg hat man dä auch gsehen /
Tausent funffhundert ists geschehen.
Vnd neunzehen Jar vmb Weinacht zeit /
Ein starck gebiß hat mich gebissen ec.

Audio hanc belluam binis dentib.
è scopulis tanquá clauo se suspendê-
tem, à Germanis Oceani litora colé-
tibus Rostinger appellari. In extrema
Moscouia, vel Hungaria Scythica, nö
longe à Tanais ortu, Morsz dicitur,
A Germanico Rusor, ( q nomé factü
videtur ab impetu & sonitu quó per
mare fertur, von dérausschen vnd grausel
àn ris égaris ex sismes, ) quidä Rosma-
rü Latina terminatione dicere volue
runt. Vel Rusor dictus est, quasi Rusor,
( nä Ru lingua nostra gigante significat, ) à magnitudine & robore pro
cæteris cü piscib. tum cetis plerisq;
præstat, Alium esse puto qui Rusval
nominatur, quinquaginta passuum
longitudine : deuorans homines &
cymbas, & inuertens naues. In luhra
& Corela Scythicis regionib. ad Sep
tétriones remotissimis, sunt aliqui
montes mediocris tumoris, qui Oce
ano per totü Septétrioné adiacêt.
Super hos scandunt ex mari pisces
Morsz nücupati, dête sese supra mö-
té cötinendo, fricando, & alcensum
pmouédo : cüq; ad summitaté môtis
puenerint, ad vlteriora gressu pmouédo, ad alterä parté montiü volutä-
do decidunt. Hos illæ gétes colligé-
do, dêtes eorü satis magnos, latôs &
albos pôdere grauissimos, capiüt, &
Moscouitis penduut atq; vendunt.
Moscouitæ vero his vtuntur ad Tattariä quoq; & Turciä mittunt, ad parandü manubria gladiorü, framea-
rü & cultrotü, quoniä grauitare sui maiore ac fortiore impressioné impingunt, & pbent impellentib. in la-
borib. pugnis, præliis, Matthias à Michon. Ceti quidä habét rictü oris dentatü prægrandib. & lögis détibus :
ita vt plerüq; inueniätur cubitales, aliquädo duorü aut trium aut quatuor cubitorü. Inter cæteros longius. p-
minent duo canini; & sunt subrus sicut cornu, imitar dentiü elephantis & apri, qui culmi vocantur. Videtur
aüt ad pugnädü esse facti, Albertus Magnus. Cöicerée aüt licet de his pcipue piscibus quos Rolmaros voca-
mus, cü sentire Et rursus, Ceti hirsuti & alii, lögissimos habét culmos, ( dentes exertos, ) & illis ad saxa in ru-
pib. se suspédut dormituri. Tü pisca tor ap. ppin quäs quatü pöt. corii a iardo subiectó separat iuxta caudä, &
funé validü immittit; qué mox ad circulos ( ferreos ) môtiu infixos, vel palos robustos vel arbores ligat. Tü
lapidib. é magna fuda proiectis caput pilces feries, excitat eu Is excitatus quä conatur recedere, pellé à cau-
da per dorsum & caput extractam relinquit. nec longe à loco illo postea debilitatus capitur : vel natus in a-
qua exanguis, vel semiuiuus iacens in litóre. S 4 Bala-

Pictura quæ Argentinæ in caldario Cieriæ visitur,
in panno expressa.

† In docto al-
cui cetus mas
risfus est, bale-
na femina :
cum cetus to-
tius generis
nomen sit, ba-
lena speciei in
vtroque sexu.

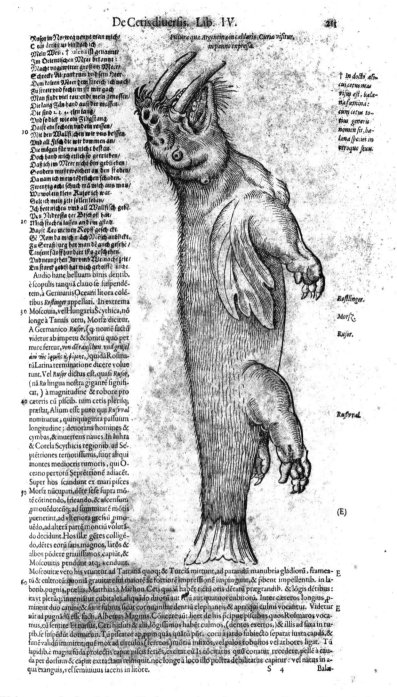

Rostinger.

Morsz.

Rusor.

Rusvval.

(E)

*Fig. 5.* Walrus as depicted by a Vatican artist, *circa* 1519. From Konrad Gesner, *Historia Animalium* (Frankfurt, 1620), book iv, p. 211. BL, 460.c.4–6

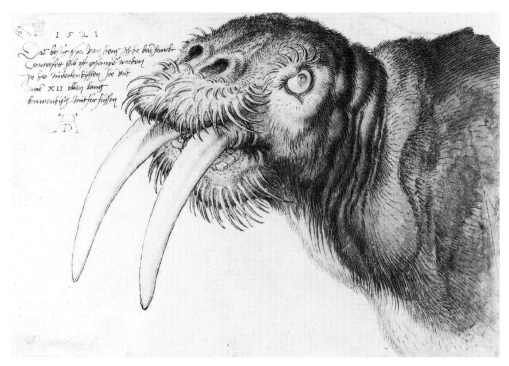

*Fig. 6.* Head of a walrus. By Albrecht Dürer, *circa* 1519 (with text added 1521). British Museum, Department of Prints and Drawings, BM. 5261–167. *By courtesy of the Trustees of the British Museum*

dumb animal whose head I have portrayed is caught in the Netherlands Sea and was 12 ells long, brownish with four feet'.[19] Nowhere on the picture itself or in his journal from his Netherlands travels did Dürer indicate that during that period he had seen and drawn a live or recently killed walrus. If he had, he would surely have shown the whole animal, and its head would have tapered smoothly from a plump neck. It would not have looked like a twin to the pathetic one in fig. 5.[20]

Dürer did not leave for the Netherlands until the summer of 1520 and could easily have indulged his interest in exotic animals with a trip to see the tusked and hairy exhibit at the Strasbourg town hall around Christmas 1519. It is also possible that the head's itinerary may have included Nuremberg.[21] The distance between the two cities is not great, and intellectual connections between them were so close that Dürer and the Nuremberg humanist, Willibald Pirckheimer, were both involved in the plans of the printer, Johann Grüninger of Strasbourg, for a post-1522 edition of Ptolemy's *Geographia*.[22] We shall return to the Strasbourg-Nuremberg nexus later, in connection with the peculiar northern 'elephant' found in various editions of Martin Waldsee-müller's *Carta marina navigatoria*, but first we must look at the genesis of Leo X's present, which exemplifies the communications web bringing news about the far north to the Habsburg Empire and Rome and is also a key to the sea monsters appearing on maps after the first two decades of the sixteenth century.

The German poem accompanying the head said the animal had been caught in Finnmark, Norway's northernmost district, and sent by the Archbishop of Nidaros in Norway. From 1510 until 1521 this position was occupied by Erik Valkendorf.[23] A letter from Valkendorf accompanied the gift to the Vatican and is still preserved in the archives there. After noting the virtues of stockfish (wind-dried cod), he described in dramatic terms the huge whales, sea serpents, and other sea monsters he had seen with his own eyes while visiting Finnmark and the mortal dangers from some of these horrors which he and his crew had weathered only because of their faith in God and St Olaf. He ended by saying that there were many other things of which he would rather not speak because they were so incredible, and because he did not wish to offend His Holiness.[24]

One wonders what he could have added to a recital worthy of Baron von Münchausen. As it was, Valkendorf's northern sea monsters haunted cartography for many generations, thanks in no small part to the receptive mind of his friend Olaus Magnus, who in 1539 made sure that readers of his *Carta marina* would be conversant with the horrors lurking in northern seas. Describing the 'dreadful animal commonly called a Rosmer', Valkendorf observes that it is from eleven to thirteen ells long and seven to eight ells wide and has a terrible head with a stiff and messy beard. The head is 'everywhere rich in teeth, but in particular it is equipped with two uncommonly large teeth in the upper jaw', of varying length but usually about one ell long. We learn that these teeth fetch a great price, especially among the Russians, and that the beast's strong, pig-like hide is likewise much in demand.

Although Valkendorf's letter does not state the year he toured the area on which so much of his income depended, the Norwegian historian Gustav Storm has calculated that the journey could only have taken place in the summer of 1512. In other words, Valkendorf could not himself have supervised the preparation of the walrus head from Finnmark in 1519. Why, then, in the same year Martin Luther's opposition to Leo X's policies reached a climax, did Valkendorf think that the salted head (with the valuable tusks intact) of a wild northern creature might cheer up the beleaguered Pope and make him look favourably upon the head of the Norwegian Church?

During this era of rapidly expanding horizons, the Pope's interest in exotica could be taken for granted, but the chief explanation for Valkendorf's action probably lies in his known friendship with Olaus Magnus, later the titular Catholic Archbishop of Uppsala and famous for his *Carta marina* as well as a history of the northern peoples published in 1555. Both of these works echo the descriptions in Valkendorf's 1519 letter, probably owing to communication between the two men. As a young priest, in 1518, Olaus was sent to the far north of Sweden to collect Peter's Pence and to sell indulgences; he is also believed to have visited the Norwegian region of Finnmark on that journey before going to Trondheim to visit Valkendorf.[25] It is very likely that Olaus Magnus arranged for the salted walrus head during his Finnmark sojourn, and that before returning to Stockholm

PLATE I

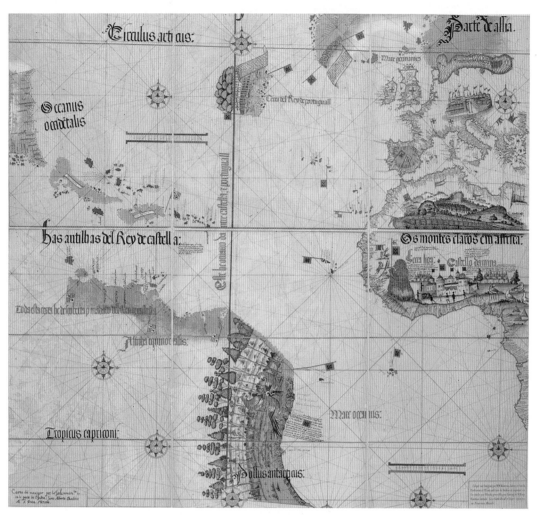

Detail from the Cantino Map of 1502 showing the southern tip of Greenland and the land discovered by the Corte Reals just to the east of the clearly drawn Tordesillas line. The original is in the Biblioteca Estense in Modena, Italy. Reproduced here from a facsimile. BL, Maps 7.e.8

PLATE II

Basque whalers harpooning their game off the Strait of Belle Isle. Detail from Pierre Descelier's 1546 World Map made for the French king. Reproduced as pl. xix in M. Jomard, *Les Monuments de la géographie* (Paris). BL, Maps Ref. A.6(1)

in 1519 he had persuaded the Norwegian archbishop – from whose jurisdiction the walrus came – to send the head to the Pope along with the letter describing the dangers and marvels of the Far North.

The reward for Olaus Magnus, in terms of papal favour gained without the appearance of blatant sycophancy, would have been in arranging for his older brother Johannes (at that time living in Rome) to deliver the gift in person to the Pope. If this was the plan, it appears to have worked. The same year Leo X received his walrus head and the world of learning gained an eyewitness description of sea monsters from such a respectable source, Johannes Magnus returned home with an appointment as papal legate.[26] And not only the Pope and the residents of Rome, but many educated and influential Germans (Albrecht Dürer among them), had had their attention drawn to the marine animal whose tusks had for centuries been the northern equivalent of elephant ivory, but with whose actual appearance no less a cartographer than Martin Waldseemüller had struggled mightily.

For his 1516 *Carta marina navigatoria*, Waldseemüller included an elephant-like creature, seen in fig. 7, with a legend explaining that this *morsus* with two long and quadrangular teeth congregated in northern Norway. Waldseemüller placed it in 'Norbegia', an area separated by a solid mountain chain from Pilappia, Lappia, and Sweden.[27] When Laurentius Fries revised this map for a new edition of Ptolemy's *Geographia* published in Strasbourg in 1522, Waldseemüller was dead and could not comment on the fact that Fries had moved the *morsus* into the open water directly north-west of Greenland.[28] To the south-west of Greenland there is a suggestion of land (unnamed); to the south of this again, beyond a large body of water, lies the 'Terra Papagalli' (Land of the Parrots), or South America.

Why did Fries move the *morsus* into what may be interpreted as the Davis Strait? The change was not necessary to achieve visual balance. Equally baffling is the fact that the *morsus* is back in northern Norway in the subsequent 1525 German edition of the *Geographia* (reprinted in 1527, 1530, and 1531) in which Fries assisted, and to which from Nuremberg both Pirckheimer and Dürer had at first objected.[29] Fries's idea of where Greenland began and ended was probably as hazy as everyone else's at the time, but it is clear that he knew the *morsus* was an aquatic creature. Had he also learned, some time before 1522, that it was not confined to northern Norway but had been caught in the northern waters frequented by 'fishermen' going to the New World? It would not be surprising if he had, because walrus ivory was valuable only if it could be marketed, and, as will shortly become evident, that particular trade had long gone through the same Flanders markets which became a crossroads for both Portuguese and South German commerce in the first quarter of the sixteenth century.

It is hard to believe that neither Fries nor Waldseemüller knew about Leo X's walrus head, or about the value of walrus ivory. Fries was a citizen of Strasbourg by 1520, where the salted head had so recently been exhibited, and the circle around his publisher Grüninger included both Dürer and Pirckheimer in Nuremberg. But despite these men's shared interests and their likely access to similar kinds of information, we cannot assume

13

*Fig. 7.* Detail of Martin Waldseemüller's 1516 *Carta marina navigatoria*, showing an elephant-like *morsus* (walrus) in northern Norway. From a facsimile in the British Library Map Library (Maps *920.(536.))

that they always shared their knowledge among themselves. We do not even know if Fries knew Waldseemüller personally; the modern cartographical scholar, Robert W. Karrow, thinks that the two men may have met when Fries came to Strasbourg to consult with Grüninger about the publication of his medical work *Spiegel der Artzney* in 1517 or 1518, when Grüninger is also known to have been working on maps and drawings for Waldseemüller's projected treatise *Chronica mundi*.[30]

Fries was trained as a physician and in that capacity may well have been welcome in the ailing cartographer's house; perhaps Waldseemüller confided some of his new ideas to Fries when he realized he would not be able to complete the *Chronica mundi* himself. Work on the *Chronica* evidently came to a standstill in 1518, presumably because of Waldseemüller's ill health, but before he died (around 1520) he had managed to complete several new drawings and to gather much new information. Some of this information Fries used in the *Uslegung*, his 1525 commentary on re-edited Ptolemy maps, and he noted plans for a more comprehensive version later.[31]

The *Uslegung* sheds no light on the *morsus* mystery, but moving the creature to the west of Greenland on the 1522 map may as easily have been Waldseemüller's idea as Fries's. On his 1516 map, Waldseemüller had expressed his intention of writing more about the northern regions in general, and both he and Fries actively sought the latest knowledge about the New World. For example, sometime between 1514–15 and 1518–19, while Fries was still practising medicine in Colmar, he wrote about using a drug compounded from guayac wood (first brought back from South America in 1508) in the treatment of syphilis, and Waldseemüller's 1516 *Carta marina navigatoria* carried the first known European representation of a South American opossum.[32]

In her painstaking study of the animals depicted on many early maps, Wilma George argues convincingly that such drawings were not ornamental but informative, and she demonstrates that Waldseemüller was especially quick to show newly discovered South American animals on his maps. His failure to do the same in 1516 for the *northern* regions of the New World is of a piece with contemporary practice, which at first emphasized 'the similarity of the nearctic animals with those of the Old World, which, considering the general similarity of the regions, is not surprising'. George goes on to note that later nearctic aberrations in the form of elephants, rhinoceroses, camels, and giraffes 'may be being used as indicators of the presence, in what were mainly unexplored territories, of many unfamiliar animals'. Calling Waldseemüller's Norwegian 'elephant' in his 1516 map (fig. 7) puzzling and difficult to identify, she does not remark on its subsequent migration into the Davis Strait under Fries's direction, nor does she identify it as a walrus.[33]

When Waldseemüller first drew his *morsus*, he would have had even less information available than the artist who drew the creature in fig. 5. People knew what the common fish species looked like, because fish were usually sold whole, whether salted or fresh, but large sea mammals had to be cut up before they could be brought to market in any form. Inland Europeans were most likely to encounter seals, walruses, or whales in the form of oil. Plate II shows that even in 1546 the otherwise well-informed Dieppe cartographer Pierre Descelier confused whales and walruses and had no clear idea of either animal's appearance when he depicted American whaling off the Strait of Belle Isle.[34]

15

Once the Age of Discovery was well under way, Europeans were increasingly exposed to news about distant regions, and people like Olaus and Johannes Magnus and Erik Valkendorf contributed both information and misinformation about northernmost Europe. Below, we shall focus on some likely sources of news about the region between Greenland and North America, keeping in mind that even the best educated people had no actual knowledge of the land connections and waterways in any part of the Arctic. A henchman of King Christian II (Erik Valkendorf's secular employer) was so unclear about Greenland's location that after his release from Russian imprisonment in 1528, he told the King that the Russian Grand Duke had taken possession of two Greenland bishoprics that were part of the Dano-Norwegian realm; a statement which raises questions about just what area another sycophant of the Danish King had had in mind when he reported from Rome in 1522 that the Spaniards were sailing ever closer to Greenland and constituting a threat to King Christian's realms.[35]

Christian II had married Princess Isabella of Spain in 1515. She was the sister of Charles V as well as of Queen Leonora of Portugal, and the niece of the formidable Margaret of Austria, Regent of the Netherlands. Many letters testify to Christian's increasing dependence on these Habsburg relations and to his involvement with the financial empire of Jacob Fugger. It is therefore not surprising to learn that he happened to be in Antwerp in July 1521, when Dürer was also there and drew a portrait of him.[36] Shortly afterwards, the artist returned to Nuremberg, full of information from his travels of 1520–1 in the Netherlands and especially from the international hub of Antwerp, where learned men and royal messengers rubbed shoulders with merchants from all over Europe, the British Isles, and the Atlantic Islands.

The sea-borne and land-borne surge in Antwerp's economic importance began around 1493 and peaked in the 1520s. The spice trade's shift from Venetian to Portuguese imports was as crucial to this economic expansion as the Portuguese demand for silver and copper; the latter also led to Portugal's strong commercial alliance with South German investors such as the Fuggers, who took the commercial lead in Antwerp during the first quarter of the sixteenth century and also helped finance the Portuguese spice trade in the Far East.[37] News and gossip flowed into Antwerp as to other major commercial junctions and fanned out to centres of learning and cartography all over Europe, in a form dictated not only by the lips that spoke, but by the ears that heard and the questions that were asked. Antwerp would have been a prime centre for early information about Portuguese activities in North America, because the Portuguese Azores (the home of such early explorers in the North Atlantic and the Davis Strait as João Fernandes and the De Barcelos and Corte Real families, and of the would-be settler Alvaro Fagundes) had a Flemish mercantile élite linking these wheat-producing islands with the Flanders grain market.[38]

Besides wheat, other basic goods such as fish, cloth, and hides were still important to the prosperity of the Antwerp market, to which both Iberian and English merchants flocked. Neither walrus tusks nor walrus hide (for heavy-duty ropes) had lost their appeal by the sixteenth century, and it is safe to assume that Antwerp merchants still knew how to market both products. In the fourteenth century, when the Norse Greenlanders paid their tithes in walrus ivory, the Norwegian authorities had depended on Flanders merchants to market this specialized commodity.[39] When the Dutch explorer Willem Barent sailed around the north of Norway to the Novaya Zemlya region in 1594, his greedy crew knew that walrus tusks were as valuable as elephant ivory.[40]

Oils extracted from the livers of cod and Greenland shark or from the blubber of seals, walruses and whales were also in strong demand, along with the flesh of the same creatures. These needs fuelled the Iberian, French and English 'fishing' ventures to North America. However, the hunt for whales and walrus would have tempted their pursuers much farther north into the Davis Strait than fishermen needed to go just to fill their ships with cod and halibut. The Basques, who gradually took up transatlantic whaling and set up the first try-works ashore in Labrador, deserve a closer look in conjunction with their quarry because of the information their activities may have provided for Portuguese and Portuguese-inspired maps.

Although both Portuguese and French fishermen had been fishing cod off 'Terranova' since 1504–5, the first written record we have of a distinctly Basque involvement dates from 1517. The first document alluding to a cargo of whale meat from Newfoundland is dated 22 March 1530, and even this cargo appears to have consisted mostly of codfish. Other early documents from Bordeaux show that when the Basques first added transatlantic whaling to their traditional whaling along the Galician and Asturian coasts, they sold the salted meat to the French specifying only that the barrels contained neither flippers nor tails, regardless of the source of their catch.[41]

Barkham notes that the Basques normally hunted right whales off their own coasts from October to March and gradually expanded their hunting season to seven months, from June to January, to accommodate the different migratory patterns of the right whales and the bowhead whales which became the whalers' prime targets in the New World.[42] Her information is crucial, because the habits and migratory patterns of these two species of whale are as important to finding out where these early whalers went as to knowing when they went. Such knowledge is central to any discussion of how far north Europeans had sailed in the Davis Strait at the time of Sebastian Cabot's preoccupation with finding the north-west passage to Cathay, and before Martin Frobisher (on a similar errand) went to Baffin Island in 1576 and found signs that the Eskimos had met white men before.

Rich in blubber and given to feeding near the surface, the northern right whale (*Eubalaena glacialis*) got its name because it was considered the 'right' target, a view that almost caused the extinction of the species. In their heyday, right whales ranged through the cooler waters of the northern hemisphere, so that in the summer season whalers could have found their quarry as far north as the entrance to Hudson Bay, overlapping with the southern range limit of a close cousin, the bowhead whale (*Balaena mysticetus*). As good a source of blubber as the right whale, and just as slow-moving and unaggressive, the bowhead whale made an even more desirable target because its baleen (an extremely useful commodity in pre-plastic days) was the longest of any whale. Bowhead whales spend all their lives at the edge of the Arctic ice and were once found throughout the northern circumpolar region. They follow the retreating ice north in the summer and swim south – but not very far south – when the new-formed ice advances.[43]

Early whaling crews ready to exploit the Labrador coast were unlikely to shy away from pursuing their game far to the north when necessary. Their profession guaranteed that they were hardy sailors anxious to earn as much as possible from their dangerous way of life, and to hunt the valuable bowhead in the Davis Strait they were obliged to go far enough north to reach the edge of the pack ice. A northwards quest might also provide access to narwhal (*Monodon monoceros*), another denizen of the Arctic likely to go south to the Hudson Strait in the summer which would certainly have been worth pursuing for its long spiral tusk. Sold for centuries in the European markets as unicorn horns with magic and medicinal power, narwhal tusks had such a reputation that when the second Frobisher expedition (1577) found 'a great deade fishe...hauyng a horne of two yardes long' in Baffin Island, George Best observed that it 'maye truely be thoughte to be the sea unicorne'. The precious horn was 'to be seene and reserued as a Jewel, by the Queens maiesties commaundement, in hir Wardrop of robes'.[44]

Also commercially significant was a third species preferring life at the edge of moving pack ice and in chilly coastal waters, namely the walrus, especially the female walrus.[45] Sixteenth-century whalers in North America would have found plenty of walrus in the Gulf of St Lawrence as well as off Cape Breton Island and Sable Island if they arrived early in the spring or stayed late into the fall. In summer, however, the animals would have retreated north along with the ice floes on which they could haul up when away from land. Walrus are common seasonally along the southern coast of Baffin Island and present the year round in the western part of Hudson Bay; until recently they probably also populated the entire eastern coast of Baffin Island as well as areas to the north.[46]

The Davis Strait narrows considerably at the Arctic Circle before widening again into Baffin Bay, and the distance between the coastal shallows of Canada and Greenland, on which the walrus depend for their food, is small. Consequently, this is where groups of walrus are most likely to be found in mid-strait, at the edge of the summer pack ice forming somewhere to the north of the narrowing.[47] It is also, as will be discussed below, likely to be the northernmost American region which Sebastian Cabot depicted on his 1544 map. In addition, it is the stretch where sixteenth-century mariners sailing up the North American coast would have been most likely to cross under the impression that they were still in 'Terranova' (North America). Sailing from Cape Dyer, the easternmost point of Baffin Island, directly across to Itilleq in Greenland, would have taken a ship right to the region favoured by Eskimos and medieval Norse Greenlanders alike for its wealth of fish and game. There is both written and archaeological evidence that some Europeans followed precisely such a route in the decades before Frobisher's voyages.

A find made during excavations in 1990–2 in south-east Greenland, about 300 km.

south of Ammassalik, has a possible bearing on early fishing and whaling in the Davis Strait as well as on discoveries made by Frobisher's men on the Greenland side. A drop-shaped red earring, from a Thule Eskimo house estimated (on the basis of a preliminary C-14 dating of a charcoal sample) to have been used A.D. 1430–1555, turns out to have been made from a European red clay tile.[49] Red roof tiles were standard in the early Basque try-works in Labrador and have been found in early Thule house ruins as far north as Hamilton Inlet, but the presence of terracotta in southeastern Greenland before the second half of the sixteenth century raises the question of how far the piece had travelled, and of whether this red earring has any connection with the 'certayne redde Hearings [earrings]' Frobisher's men found in 1578 in an Eskimo tent on the west coast of Greenland. In addition to the earrings, the Englishmen observed a box of iron nails and 'dyuers other things artificially wroughte, whereby it appeareth, that [the Eskimos] haue trade with some ciuill people, or else are in deede themselves artificiall workmen'.[49]

On Baffin Island, too, Frobisher and his men found indications that other Europeans had been there before them. A doublet and European-style boots found in an Eskimo tent merely served to convince them that five of their own crew from the previous year had come to grief, but George Best thought pieces of iron and copper bars showed that the natives 'vse to traffike and exchange their commodities with some other people ...'. We get a fair idea of who these 'other people' may have been when Best continues: 'We found also in their tents a Guinney Beane, of redde couloure, the which dothe vsually grow in the hote Countreys: whereby it appéereth they trade with other Nations whiche dwelle farre off, or else themselues are great travellers'.[50] Portuguese trade with Guinea was by this time more than a century old. A Basque or Portuguese crew may well have brought red Guinea beans along as food and discovered that the North American natives found them as ornamental as the small glass beads the Portuguese usually brought along for trade. One thing is certain: the bean could only have reached Baffin Island with a European ship some time after about 1500, because the Norse Greenlanders had never raised anything remotely similar; that ship would most likely have been Basque or Portuguese. English and French fishermen seem to have concentrated their efforts somewhat farther south; the little we know of English efforts to find the north-west passage in the first half of the sixteenth century does not suggest efforts to trade with Baffin Island Eskimos; Jacques Cartier's penetration into the St Lawrence region channelled post-1534 French efforts away from areas farther north; Spanish interests in America lay to the south and west; the Dutch had not yet begun whaling in the Davis Strait; and the European recolonization of Greenland did not begin until 1721.

In Best's comment that the bean might be proof of Eskimo contact with distant countries we find an echo of Frobisher's original goal of finding the north-west passage to Cathay. Fishing and whaling were never part of his brief, any more than for his fellow countrymen Sebastian Cabot and Robert Thorne the younger, or for Jacques Cartier and other Europeans who, armed with royal licences, had probed the Davis Strait after 1500.

While there is good reason to suppose that Basque and Portuguese fishermen and whalers quietly pursued their North American business from the very beginning of the sixteenth century, there is a noticeable lack of official Portuguese ventures into the Davis Strait after 1503. By that time, the disappearance of the brothers Gaspar and Miguel Corte Real and the Portuguese success in establishing a reliable sea route to India around Africa probably put a low priority on finding a north-west passage.

We know little about the Corte Real brothers' sailing routes, the regions they discovered, where and how they met their end, and what their goal had been.[51] Written sources as well as the Cantino map of 1502 (Plate I) suggest that they sailed around Cape Farewell in Greenland and found land with tall trees and other pleasant attributes somewhere in the southern Labrador-Newfoundland-Nova Scotia region, but there is nothing to tell us how far north they had sailed before being deterred and forced westwards by ice. We cannot even be certain that this ice was in the Davis Strait rather than in the Denmark Strait between Iceland and the east coast of Greenland.

However, we can be reasonably sure that, as wealthy courtiers rather than fishermen, the Corte Reals hoped to find a passage to Cathay through obstacles whose shape and name they did not and could not know at such an early date, and that they and their crew were familiar with the traditional European sailing route to Iceland. That was the codfish route, and it is shown with stunning accuracy and simplicity in the Cantino map. Scholars usually assume that the legend by Cape Farewell in Greenland is as direct a tribute to the Corte Reals as the one by the wooded island called 'Terra del Rey de portuguall', but the cartographer did not actually name the subjects of the Portuguese king who had discovered what we know as Cape Farewell, which by 1500 must have been a well-known reference point for English and Iberian navigators in the north-west Atlantic.[52]

Although the Gemma Frisius-Mercator (Zerbst) globe of *circa* 1537 supposedly drew on Portuguese information, the North Atlantic and North American delineations in this work are a sharp contrast to the informed realism of the 1502 Cantino map and are perhaps as good an illustration as any of where a mostly cerebral approach to cartography might lead during the period under discussion here. This globe featured a wide northern strait cutting north-west through a massive and unrealistic North American land mass to connect the Atlantic and the Pacific Oceans.[53] The legend stated that this was the 'Strait of the Three Brothers, through which Portuguese attempted to sail to the Orient and the Indies and the Moluccas' and is generally believed to refer to Gaspar, Miguel, and Vasco Annes Corte Real. Although the distinguished Cabot scholar James A. Williamson expressed some doubt about that interpretation,[54] it makes better sense to connect the legend with the Corte Reals than with the Cabots. Of the three Cabot brothers, only Sebastian, who never gave credit to others if he could help it, was likely to have been known to Gemma Frisius and Mercator. It is also reasonable to see the strait as illustrating a claimed Portuguese knowledge of a north-west passage which, in harmony with the Treaty of Tordesillas, sliced off a large area of new territory to the north and north-east of a version of the Davis Strait based on wishful thinking. But nowhere is there any indication at all that Frisius had sought, or had access to, recent first-hand experience of the New World. His sources of information seem even more doubtful when

20

we look at the legend off the north-western shore of that supposed north-west passage: 'These are the people reached by John Scolvus a Dane about the year 1476'.[55] This is not the place to unwind the many yarns subsequently spun around 'Scolvus the Dane', but it needs to be said that in the year 1476 the Danes were not sending expeditions to either Greenland or North America. Deep in financial and political troubles in Europe, the Danish crown had long ceased to care about its ancient Norwegian colony in Greenland and had not yet been piqued by the new American discoveries.

While English and continental cosmographers struggled to imagine our earth, one Englishman in particular preferred to test theory, of which he had plenty, by action, of which he saw more than most, but not as much as he would have liked. Until his death at a ripe old age in 1557, Sebastian Cabot was convinced that either to the east above Norway or to the west through North America there must be a short northern route to Cathay. His map of 1544 (northern section in fig. 4) indicates that he had been old enough to accompany his father to North America in 1497; he certainly sailed to Newfoundland in 1504 with Robert Thorne and Hugh Elyot of Bristol, who had equipped two ships for a transatlantic voyage which seems to have had both fishing and exploration as its goal.[56]

We do not know how far north or south they went at that time, but Sebastian Cabot evidently saw enough to convince him that he needed to look farther north. When he headed up into the Davis Strait on an expedition of his own lasting from 1508 until 1509, he most likely knew, either from personal experience or from Waldseemüller's 1507 World Map, that he was dealing with a separate American continent, but he could have had little inkling of its shape and size. Fortunately, he would have brought with him the best available knowledge of the North American coast besides his own, for his Bristol crew (reportedly about 300 men) would probably have included both Englishmen who had fished far up along the Labrador coast and Portuguese mariners with similar experience.[57]

Various reports written within about forty years of Sebastian Cabot's first independent voyage agree in two respects: he had sailed far enough up into the Davis Strait to encounter drift ice in July, causing his mate and crew to threaten mutiny, and he had eventually coasted back down the coast to the 'Baccalaos' region and beyond.[58] The latitudes he reached and the manoeuvres he made are reported so variously that we are none the wiser. It is equally impossible to distinguish in these accounts, which are all second-hand, what constituted self-advertisement on Cabot's part and what reflected the wishes and theories of the authors themselves. There are nevertheless several reasons to believe that he had sailed past Cape Dyer at the narrowing of the Davis Strait and into Baffin Bay, far enough north to reach the receding edge of the summer pack ice during a period notable for a slight warming trend.[59]

First of all, Cabot's aim was to explore farther north than either he or his crew had been before, and it is likely that a long stretch of the Labrador coast would have been familiar to some of them by that time. Common sense suggests that a mate and crew accustomed to fishing and sailing in those northern waters, exactly the kind of men

Sebastian Cabot would have hired, would not threaten mutiny unless they were in unfamiliar waters and conditions were unusually terrible. Secondly, we know that the medieval Norse Greenlanders had sailed as far north as the seventy-third parallel, and there is no reason to suppose that Sebastian Cabot and his men were less hardy or worse equipped than they.[60] Thirdly and most importantly, Sebastian Cabot's own map suggests that he crossed the Arctic Circle and sailed past Cape Dyer. Allowing for likely interpolations, the statements made by other people whom Sebastian Cabot had told about his voyages support the story.[61]

Sebastian Cabot was long since dead, after spending his sunset years back home in England and making repeated personal and vicarious attempts to find the fabled short cut, when Sir Humphrey Gilbert argued in favour of a north-west passage and wrote (1576):[62]

Furthermore, Sebastian Cabots [sic] by his personal experience and travel hath set foorth, and described this passage in his Charts, which are yet to be seene in the Queens Majesties Privie Gallerie at Whitehall, who was sent to make this discovery by king Henry the seventh, and entered the same fret: affirming that he sayled very farre Westward, with a quarter of the North, on the Northside of Terra de Labrador the eleventh of June, until he came to the Septentrionall latitude of 67 degrees and a halfe, and finding the Seas still open, sayd, that he might, & would have gone to Cataia, if the mutinie of the Master and Mariners had not bene.

Richard Willes summoned both Gemma Frisius and Sebastian Cabot in his own 1577 arguments for the existence of a north-west passage.[63] He noted that Sebastian Cabot had

entred personally that streiete, sent by King Henry the seventh to make this aforesaid discovery, as in his owne discourse of navigation you may reade in his carde drawen with his owne hands, the mouth of the north-westerne streict lieth neare the 318 Meridian, betwixt 61. and 64. degrees in elevation, continuying the same breadth about 10. degrees west, where it openeth southerly more and more, untyll it come under the tropike of Cancer, and so runneth into Mar de Zur ...

Since Sebastian Cabot never claimed to have gone the whole way through to Cathay, we may safely consider Willes's statement about the fortuitous southern termination of the 'streiete' a reflection of his belief in the 'Strait of the Three Brothers' as depicted by Frisius, which made the Pacific accessible via the earth's northern regions. Sebastian Cabot's own map tells a very different story. It depicts no clear passage through the North American continent between the sixty-first and sixty-fourth parallels or anywhere else; instead, it shows the North American coast as it continues north-east from the St Lawrence, reaching its easternmost point just below the Polar Circle and continuing some way to the north-west before it peters out in the 'Frozen Sea' at the top. Willes's description has been interpreted as evidence that Sebastian had entered the Hudson Strait and sailed into Hudson Bay.[64] The description of a northern strait angling to the west before opening up again into a broad expanse of water fits the Davis Strait transition into Baffin Bay equally well, however, and that possibility is certainly more in keeping with the map in fig. 4.

It is a pity that not even the 'Charts...to be seene in the Queens Majesties Privie Gallerie at Whitehall' survive to tell us how consistent Sebastian Cabot's map delineations were overall. Since the cartographic information about Norway with which he dispatched poor Willoughby and Chancellor to find the north-east passage in 1553 was hopelessly inadequate, the outline in fig. 4 probably represents the best he could do with a region he had never visited, and with which contemporary European cartographers were no help. The Davis Strait, on the other hand, he knew by personal experience and through years spent in the company of mariners from Bristol and elsewhere, both before and after his 1508–9 voyage. Added to this were his many years in Spanish service, which had given him full access to the closely guarded 'Padrón real' (the royal master map), whose influence the map in fig. 4 also demonstrates.[65]

As a cosmographer and navigator Sebastian Cabot received mixed reviews among both his contemporaries and later historians, and modesty seems not to have been a conspicuous part of his personality. He nevertheless accomplished much and, at the age of sixty or so, is unlikely to have jeopardized his reputation by making a map that failed to show all that he knew. If we assume that when he drew the map in fig. 4 he had a clear idea about the latitudes of places he himself had visited in North and South America, and if we accept his own depictions and descriptions of those areas just as they are, several conclusions suggest themselves.

Before Sebastian Cabot was born at Venice, Bristol men had known that by sailing home along the fifty-third parallel, with the wind and the current at their stern, they were likely to reach Galway safely. Sebastian Cabot correctly placed the entrance to the St Lawrence at about that latitude, with the major cod fisheries shown to the south and south-east. Williamson's arguments that John Cabot had coasted well to the south of Newfoundland on his voyage of 1497, possibly making a landfall in Maine, therefore seem borne out.[66] So do the claims of Robert Thorne the Younger in 1527 (fig. 3) that before John Cabot's 1497 voyage, his father and Hugh Elyot had laid claim to the coast of 'Noua terra Laboratorum dicta (The New Land called Labrador)', which Thorne shows lying farthest north, and which at that time is likely to have included not only the northern part of modern Labrador, but also a part of western Greenland. It would not be surprising if both Sebastian Cabot and Robert Thorne had a good notion of where their fathers had gone in earlier years, seen in relation to the slowly evolving picture of the North American coast.

The strong eastward trend of that coastline presented great problems for even the most honest cartographers and explorers, however, because of their inability to calculate longitude accurately. This handicap made east-west distances peculiarly liable to the kind of distortion we find in the coast north of the St Lawrence in fig. 4 and in other maps of the period. Arriving at proper delineations for this seaboard was made even more difficult by the problem of compass deviation, which increased the farther north one went. Calculating latitude, however, was easier, and it is therefore significant that on his map, Sebastian Cabot placed the Arctic Circle (66°17′ N) where he thought it belonged: near the easternmost promontory marking the entrance to what seemed to be a widening north-west passage. On modern maps, the equivalent promontory is called Cape Dyer, and the 'passage' would be the capacious but ice-plagued Baffin Bay, reached through a shorter and less menacing approach than the access provided to Hudson Bay by the Hudson Strait. If the widening waters of Baffin Bay were what Sebastian saw in 1508, it explains why he was haunted for the rest of his life by the conviction that this was a sea lane to Asia. But to those engaged in the 'common and usuall trade' provided by those chilly waters, and from whom he must have learned much, such dreams probably seemed as unimportant as their own daily grind was to the learned world.

1 See, e.g., David B. Quinn, *England and the Discovery of America* (London, 1974); David B. Quinn, Alison M. Quinn, and Susan Hillier (eds.), *New American World: A Documentary History of North America to 1612* (New York, 1979), vol. i, p. 91; A. A. Ruddock, 'The Reputation of Sebastian Cabot', *Bulletin of the Institute of Historical Research*, xlvii (1974), p. 98.

2 Grethe Authén Blom in *Kulturhistorisk Leksikon for Nordisk Middelalder*, vol. iv (1959), cols. 281–7; Odd Vollan, op. cit., vol. xviii (1974), cols. 506–10.

3 Claudius Ptolemaeus, *Geographia* (Rome, 1508); BL, Maps C.1.d.5 and 6.

4 See Donald L. McGuirk, Jr., 'Ruysch World Map: Census and Commentary', *Imago Mundi*, xli (1989), for a close study of several important changes Ruysch made in his plates.

5 Quinn, Quinn, and Hillier, vol. i, pp. 103, 154; A. A. Ruddock, 'The Reputation of Sebastian Cabot', pp. 95–9; D. B. Quinn, *North America from Earliest Discoveries to First Settlements* (London, 1975), pp. 129–30.

6 Francisco López de Gómara, *Historia de las Indias* (first published Seville, 1553), as quoted in Henry Harrisse, *The Discovery of America* (London, 1892), vol. i, p. 131.

7 E. G. R. Taylor, 'A Letter dated 1577 from Mercator to John Dee', *Imago Mundi*, xiii (1956), pp. 56–67; Richard Hakluyt, *The Principall Navigations, Voiages and Discoveries of the English Nation*, facsimile ed. of London, 1589 ed., introduced by David B. Quinn and R. A. Skelton and indexed by Alison Quinn (Cambridge, 1965), vol. i, p. 249. For an analysis of Nicholas of Lynn and *Inventio Fortunata*, see K.

A. Seaver, *The Frozen Echo* (Stanford, California, 1996), chapter v.

8 Hakluyt, *The Principall Navigations*, vol. i, p. 268.

9 For the first seven decades or so of the sixteenth century, the name Labrador was most often applied to what we know as Greenland. See James A. Williamson, *The Cabot Voyages and Bristol Discovery under Henry VII* (London, 1962), pp. 98, 120–1, 312–17.

10 Ibid., pp. 309–11. For a further discussion of 'the sea discovered by the English', see Seaver, chs. ix, x.

11 Richard Hakluyt, *The Principal Navigations ... of the English Nation* (Glasgow, 1903), vol. ii, pp. 159–81 (the map is between pp. 176–7).

12 Letter of 18 Dec. 1497 from Raimondo de Soncino to the Duke of Milan, *Calendar of State Papers. Milan*, pp. 336–7; Williamson, pp. 209–11.

13 Seaver, chs. vii–x. Sailing east on about the fifty-third parallel would take a ship back to the Irish port of Galway, which the Bristol men frequented.

14 Gesner's four-volume illustrated *Historia Animalium* included wild and domestic creatures of land, sea, and sky and was published in a variety of Latin editions and in a German translation. Marine creatures constitute bk iv. I have primarily used the *Fischbuch* of 1575.

15 Selma H. Barkham, *Los vascos en el marco Atlantico Norte, siglos XVI y XVII*, vol. iii of ITSASOA, gen. ed. Enrique Ayerbe (Bilbao, 1987), pp. 28–30, 39, 58–60; *Diplomatarium Islandicum*, vol. xvi, no. 240, letter of 5 Mar. 1499 from De Puebla to Queen Isabella (source: *Calendar of State Papers. Spanish* [London,

1862], vol. ii b, no. 233). As late as 1862, the American explorer Charles Francis Hall wondered, 'is a whale a fish?', *Life with the Esquimaux* (London, 1864), p. 21.

16 Charles Lethbridge Kingsford (ed.), *Chronicles of London* (Oxford, 1905), p. 167. 'Walrus' reproduced from Konrad Gesner, *Historia Animalium* (Frankfurt, 1620), bk. iv, p. 211; in the 1575 *Thierbuch*, the information and picture appear in bk. iv, p. 48. For the *Carta marina*, see facsimile BL, Maps 184.e.1, Plate B.

17 For more information on this drawing and the one in fig. 6, see Valentin Kiparsky, 'L'Histoire du morse', *Annales Academiae Scientiarum Fennicae*, lxxiii, Series B (1952), no. 3, pp. 46–7.

18 'Head of a Walrus', British Museum, Department of Prints and Drawings, BM. 5261–167.

19 German text: 'Das dosig thyr van dem jch do das hawbt/contrefett hab ist gefangen worden/jn die niederlendischen see vnd/was XII ellen lang mit fur fussen'. John Rowlands, *The Age of Dürer and Holbein: German Drawings 1400–1550* (London, 1988), pp. 102–3, translates this as 'that stupid animal ... was caught in the Netherlands Sea', but Prof. Orrin W. Robinson III at Stanford University, California, thought that Dürer's mixing of tenses here is probably of no great moment, being common practice at the time.

20 There is still no information on the date or occasion for the drawing. Dürer often took his pictures along when travelling and had a habit of making later notations on his works. (Pers. comm. in Jan. 1995 by Giulia Bartrum, Assistant Keeper, British Museum, Department of Prints and Drawings.)

21 Kiparsky, pp. 46–8.

22 Robert W. Karrow, Jr., *Mapmakers of the Sixteenth Century and their Maps* (Chicago, 1993), p. 199; Meret Petrzilka, *Die Karten des Laurent Fries von 1530 und 1531 und ihre Vorlage, die 'Carta Marina' aus dem Jahre 1516 von Martin Waldseemüller*, Zurich dissertation (pressmarked Maps 203.d.26), pp. 14–20.

23 *Diplomatarium Norvegicum*, vol. xvii, no. 1259; vol. i, no. 1059; vol. vii, no. 558, etc.

24 K. H. Karlsson and Gustav Storm (eds.), 'Finnmarkens Beskrivelse af Erkebiskop Erik Walkendorf', *Det Norske Geografiske Selskabs Aarbog*, xii (1902), pp. 1–24. It has the Latin text and a Norwegian translation of the letter, as well as valuable comments by Storm. Bk. x describes the 'Rosmer'.

25 Karl Ahlenius, *Olaus Magnus och hans framställning af Nordens Geografi* (Uppsala, 1895), pp. 39–44; Lars Hamre, *Erkebiskop Erik Valkendorf. Trekk av hans liv og virke* (Oslo, 1943), p. 39.

26 Johannes Magnus became archbishop in 1524. A good source of pertinent dates is Robert W. Karrow, Jr., *Mapmakers of the Sixteenth Century and their Maps*, p. 362.

27 Martin Waldseemüller, *Carta marina navigatoria*, 1516, in facsimile, Maps *920.(536).

28 Ptolemy, *Geographia*, ed. Laurentius Fries (Strasbourg, 1522); Maps C.1.d.11.

29 Petrzilka, pp. 19–24, with fold-out maps; Karrow, pp. 194–202, 572–83.

30 Karrow, p. 193.

31 Ibid., pp. 193–9.

32 Ibid., p. 191; Wilma George, *Animals and Maps*, with a preface by Helen Wallis (Berkeley, California, 1969), pp. 61–2.

33 George, esp. pp. 61–3, 83, 86–7, 101, 119.

34 Detail from Pierre Descelier's 1546 World Map, made for the French King. From M. Jomard, *Les Monuments de la géographie* (BL, Maps Ref. 6.A), pl. xix.

35 *Diplomatarium Norvegicum*, vol. xi, pp. 603–5; vol. xiv, no. 627; Hamre, p. 48 (citing *Acta Pontifica Danica*, vol. vi, no. 4895).

36 See, e.g., *Diplomatarium Norvegicum*, vol. xvii, no. 1262; Rowlands, pp. 102–6.

37 Herman van der Wee, *The Growth of the Antwerp Market and the European Economy* (The Hague, 1963), vol. ii, pp. 113–45; idem, 'European Long-Distance Trade, 1350–1750', in James D. Tracy (ed.), *The Rise of Merchant Empires* (Cambridge, 1990), p. 29.

38 Felipe Fernández-Armesto, *Before Columbus. Exploration and Colonization from the Mediterranean to the Atlantic 1229–1492* (Philadelphia, 1987), pp. 198–200.

39 See, e.g., *Diplomatarium Norvegicum*, vol. xix, no. 459.

40 The Dutchmen just did not know enough about the animals to kill a single one of about two hundred walrus they found basking in the sun. Erik van Mingroot and Eduard van Ermen, *Scandinavia in Old Maps and Prints*, trans. by Tony MacKrill (Knokke, 1987), p. 63.

41 Barkham, pp. 11–12 (prefatory remarks by Iñaki Zumalde), 28–37.

42 Ibid., p. 30.

43 Erich Hoyt, *The Whales of Canada* (Camden East, Ontario, 1984), pp. 50–62.

44 Ibid., pp. 84–9; Vilhjalmur Stefansson and Eloise McCaskill, *The Three Voyages of Martin Frobisher* (London, 1938), vol. i, p. 62.

45 An average female walrus yields over 150 lbs of hide and has more blubber per pound of body weight than a male, and the females' tusks have the finer grain. Furthermore, females are easier to hunt. They and their pups stay closer to the edge of the drift ice, making them more accessible to hunters in boats, while the males tend to go farther in. Erik W. Born, Mads P. Heide-Jørgensen, and Rolph A. Davis, 'The Atlantic Walrus (*Odobenus rosmarus rosmarus*) in West Greenland', *Meddelelser om Grønland, Bioscience*, xl (1994), pp. 4, 22–5. This excellent new study has maps and diagrams of walrus populations and seasonal migrations on both sides of the Davis Strait.

46 Randall R. Reeves, *Atlantic Walrus (Odobenus rosmarus rosmarus). A Literature Survey and Status Report*, U.S. Department of the Interior Fish and Wildlife Service, Research Report no. x (Washington, D.C., 1978), pp. 13–22.

47 Born, Jørgensen, and Davis, p. 12, fig. 5.

48 Hans Christian Gulløv and Minik Rosing, 'Kong Frederik den Sjettes Kyst – glimt fra tre somres undersøgelser i Østgrønland', *Fra National-museets Arbejdsmark*, 1993, p. 78; Hans Christian Gulløv, 'Thulekulturen i Sydøstgrønland – set fra Skjoldungen', *Forskning i Grønland/tusaat* (1994), nos. 1–2, p. 24.

49 Stefansson and McCaskill, vol. i, p. 86.

50 Ibid., vol. i, pp. 69, 126.

51 The basic documentary sources are printed in Henry Percival Biggar, *The Precursors of Cartier, 1497–1534* (Ottawa, 1911), pp. 61–7. For a useful modern commentary on the Corte Real voyages, see David B. Quinn, *England and the Discovery of America, 1481–1620*, pp. 111–18.

52 Seaver, ch. x.

53 The British Library Map Library has a set of photographs of the Zerbst globe (Maps 8.bb.10.(4.)). There is also a reproduction of the North American region in Niels Nørlund, *Danmarks Kortlægning* (Copenhagen, 1943), pl. 8.1 (Maps 19.b.19).

54 James A. Williamson, *The Cabot Voyages and Bristol Discovery under Henry VII*, p. 169. The translation of the map legend is from Samuel Eliot Morison, *The European Discovery of America* (New York, 1971), vol. i, p. 92.

55 Translated in Morison, vol. i, p. 92.

56 A. A. Ruddock, 'The Reputation of Sebastian Cabot', pp. 95–9.

57 Close connections between Portuguese (especially Azorean) entrepreneurs and local Bristol men is evident in the formation of the Anglo-Azorean Syndicate in 1501. Documents in Quinn, Quinn, and Hillier, vol. i, pp. 103–18.

58 Williamson, pp. 146–7, 266–73. Karrow, pp. 103–12, has a good recent account of Sebastian Cabot.

59 C. U. Hammer, H. B. Clausen, and W. Dansgaard, 'Greenland Ice Sheet Evidence of Post-Glacial Volcanism and its Climatic Impact', *Nature*, cclxxxviii (1980), pp. 230–5.

60 The National Museum in Copenhagen has a small, flat stone with a message in runes, carved in the early spring some time in the mid thirteenth century and proof of the Norse Greenlanders' northern probes in the course of their hunts for maritime game. The stone was found at lat. 72°57′ N on the Greenland side of Baffin Bay. For a recent discussion of this stone, see Jette Arneborg, 'Contact between Eskimos and Norsemen in Greenland', in Else Roesdal and Preben Meulengracht Sørensen (eds.), *Beretning fra tolvte tværfaglige vikingesymposium, Aarhus Universitet 1993* (Aarhus, 1993), pp. 23–35.

61 Texts reproduced in Williamson, pp. 265–91.

62 Stefansson and McCaskill, p. lxxxv.

63 The pertinent passage from Richard Willes, *The History of Travayle in the West and East Indies*, is printed in Williamson, pp. 278–9.

64 Karrow, p. 106; Williamson, pp. 167–9.

65 Ibid., p. 108.

66 Ibid., pp. 63–83.

26

# THOMAS JEFFERYS'S MAP OF CANADA AND THE MAPPING OF THE WESTERN PART OF NORTH AMERICA, 1750–1768

JOAN WINEARLS

THOMAS JEFFERYS (*c.* 1710–71), the major English engraver and map publisher of the mid-eighteenth century, is known particularly for the important maps of the eastern half of North America which he produced mainly from the early 1750s and into the 1760s. His maps of Virginia (1753), *New Map of Nova Scotia*, *North America from the French of Mr D'Anville* and New England all produced in 1755, detailed maps of Louisbourg and the St Lawrence River and South Carolina (1757), Halifax and Quebec (1758, 1759), and his involvement in the engraving and publication of some of James Cook's charts of Newfoundland in the late 1760s have been discussed at some length by various scholars.[1] But little has been said about his maps of the western areas of the continent and his approach to the mapping of the De Fonte fantasy about the purported discovery of a northwest passage from Hudson Bay to the Pacific Ocean. One of the most prominent of his later maps is the *Map of Canada and the North Part of Louisiana* (1760; see fig. 2) which was derived from the manuscript source map, 'A Map of the Northern Parts of America' (BL, K.Top.CXIX.7–2; Plate III).

As one of the first of the English map publishers to be making and publishing new maps of the west coast of the continent at mid-century, Jefferys invaded a field still largely dominated by the French. Thus, it is important to look at his maps and sources in some detail. In addition it is well known that Jefferys considered himself to be primarily an engraver (and presumably a map publisher) but only secondarily a geographer, despite his designation as Geographer to Frederick, Prince of Wales, and afterwards to George III.[2] Consequently, his mapping of the west coast and approach to the De Fonte fantasy, besides disseminating new information on various areas, throw some light on his business and professional practices and his involvement in the geography that he was portraying.

Biographical information on Thomas Jefferys is provided in considerable detail in J. B. Harley's article on his bankruptcy of 1766.[3] The exact date of his birth is not known but it may have been the second decade of the eighteenth century, extrapolating from recently discovered information about his education. It had been assumed by Harley and others that he was trained as an engraver, possibly outside the map trade, but Lawrence

27

Worms has discovered that he was apprenticed as an engraver to Emmanuel Bowen in the Merchant Taylors' Company in 1735 and thus was educated firmly in the mainstream of London map-making.[4] Nevertheless, Jefferys appears as a publisher as early as 1732, when he issued a reworking of an earlier plan of London and Westminster.[5] Harley, who notes that Jefferys has been called the most competent English cartographer and leading map and chart supplier of his day, points out that before 1750 his map-making work was limited in conception and deduces that he lacked capital. He engraved several sets of maps for books and for magazines such as Edward Caves's *Gentleman's Magazine* for which twenty maps were completed in 1746. In the same year he was appointed Geographer to Frederick, Prince of Wales. In 1749 he engraved twenty-two maps for Salmon's *A New Geographical and Historical Grammar* including one of North America, a small map showing a blank area west of the Great Lakes.[6] In conjunction with William Herbert he issued a large *Map of North America*, just after 1750 following his move to his new address at the Corner of St Martin's Lane. This map is, however, a later state of George Willdey's map of 1720 for which Jefferys or Jefferys and Herbert must have acquired the plates.[7] The geography of the west depicted on this map appears to have been lifted entirely from Guillaume Delisle's *Carte du Canada* of 1703 and shows the imaginary Long River from Lahontan and Lake 'Assenipolis' (or Assinipoils) west of the Great Lakes (an early version of Lake Winnipeg) as found on many other maps of the period.

Clearly Jefferys was acting only as an engraver or publisher and map seller for these projects and the content was provided by others. After 1750, Harley notes, Jefferys began to consolidate his position not only as a publisher and engraver but also as a major authority on the mapping of North America and in the next five years American maps began to dominate his publishing ventures. He also began to accumulate large numbers of foreign and American map sources both to sell and to use in the production of new maps. For instance, in one publication in 1755 he noted that the following American maps were 'Just Imported' from France: three maps of Canada or the world by J. N. Bellin, two maps of parts of North America by Robert de Vaugondy, one map of North America by J. B. B. D'Anville, and several atlases by Le Rouge.[8] This must have been an important part of his business in the early 1750s as there were almost no reliable British maps of North America and there was a growing demand for them in the years leading up to the Seven Years' War (1756–63) with the French. As he began compiling and publishing more and more new maps, he was clearly given access to many manuscript maps held by government departments.[9] In addition Jefferys was drawn himself into the politics of the French and English land claims in North America which meant that he put a greater investment into the production of accurate maps.[10]

As Harley notes however, Jefferys employed three main groups in his workshop: 'experts' or geographers to compile many of his new maps, and write text about them; draughtsmen to copy plans and prepare fair drawings for the engraver; and engravers.[11] However, it is doubtful, even with all of this professional support, whether as a publisher he was concerned with issuing consistent geographical information. This is nowhere

PLATE III

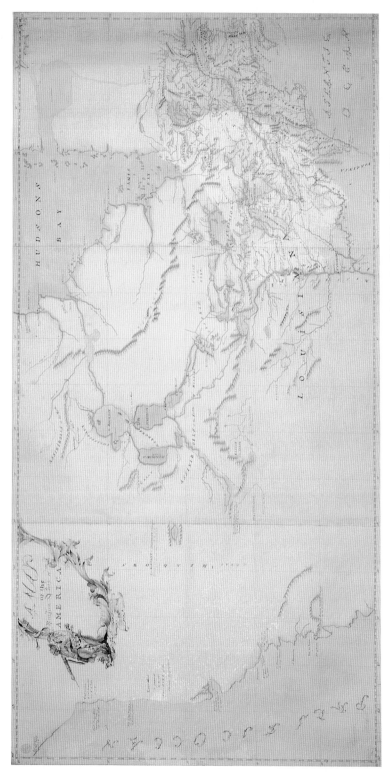

Anonymous manuscript map, 'A "Map of the Northern Parts of America"'. BL, K.Top.CXIX.7–2

PLATE IV

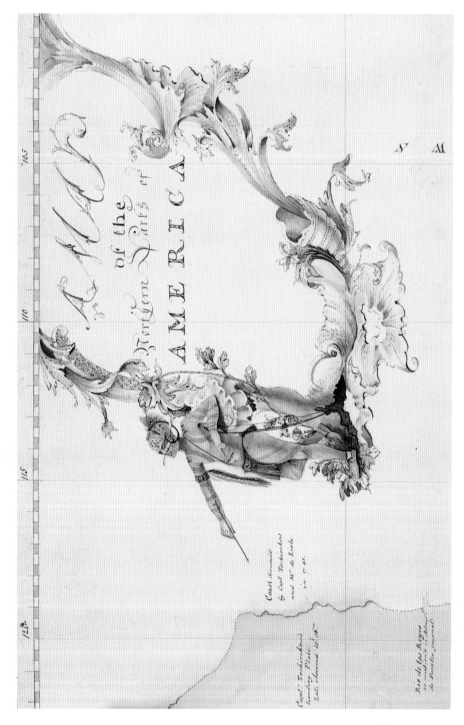

The Cartouche from 'A "Map of the Northern Parts of America"'. BL, K.Top.CXIX.7–2 (detail)

more evident than in his publishing of maps depicting the De Fonte fantasy. He frequently employed others to make new maps, well researched from various sources, but he also copied from the work of others and sometimes only engraved, printed or published the work of other authors. Jefferys's role, therefore, varied greatly from map to map and it is important to study each of these maps carefully to understand the function he played with each one.

## MAPS BY JOHN GREEN (BRADDOCK MEAD)

The first major new map published by Jefferys was the 1753 *Chart of North and South America* (see fig. 1) which he entrusted to John Green (Braddock Mead) who was a geographer of some minor repute at the time. Jefferys had met Green in 1735 when Jefferys was engraving the maps compiled by Green for the latter's translation of J. B. Du Halde's *Description of the Empire of China* published by Edward Cave (1738–41).[12] Green also edited the various volumes of the *New General Collection of Voyages and Travels* (London: Thomas Astley, 1745–7). The volume on North America in this compendium was never published, but Green's accumulated knowledge of the subject must have provided an excellent background for the maps he undertook for Jefferys in the 1750s.[13] As Harley notes, Jefferys employed Green from 1752 until his suicide in 1757, and owed a lot to him as some of his best maps were compiled by Green.[14]

The *Chart of North and South America* in six sheets published with a memoir was the first map made for Jefferys by Green and the North American area is of importance in light of Jefferys's later maps of the western part of the continent. Each sheet was issued with its own title, probably so that they could be sold separately. Sheets III & IV were the ones showing North America below 60 degrees of latitude and they were entitled appropriately. Sheet III: *Chart containing the coasts of California, New Albion and Russian discoveries to the North...* emphasized the question of the west coast and Sheet IV : *Chart of the Atlantic Ocean, with the British, French & Spanish Settlements in North America and the West Indies* dealt with the question of the possession of the eastern part of the continent. All the sheets were listed as published on 19 February 1753 and the notes about the map, although written earlier, were probably issued at the same time. Each sheet of the six-sheet chart included extensive comparative tables showing locations by the leading French cartographers J. N. Bellin and J. B. Bourgignon D'Anville as well as those by various navigators. Green used the rectangular Wright-Mercator projection and in his *Remarks* stressed the importance of it for navigational charts, while also discussing the types of projections used by various French cartographers for purposes other than navigation. He used Ferro, westernmost of the Canary Islands, as the Prime Meridian to facilitate comparison to French charts, although he also computed and showed longitudes from London along the top margin of the sheets.[15]

In discussing his sources, Green was critical of most of the French cartographers in their determination of locations and shapes of coasts, although he had to rely heavily on their work for lack of other sources. D'Anville, he noted, was wrong in his depiction of

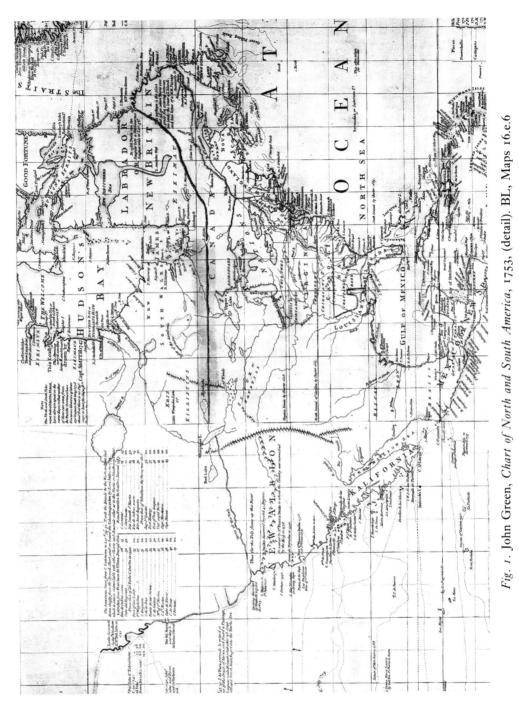

*Fig. 1.* John Green, *Chart of North and South America*, 1753, (detail). BL, Maps 16.e.6

the extent of Asia, but Green followed him for the east coast of North America more than Bellin. Green also used D'Anville for the Great Lakes rather than Bellin who, he said, placed them too far west and north to favour the latter's theory of communication with the Pacific.[16] Furthermore, Green noted that Bellin made gross mistakes by relying on poor observations of latitude and rejecting recent journals of discovery. He reviewed these sources but clearly for these two sheets of the *Chart* rejected much of Bellin's work. Green further noted that on the west coast of America there were no accurate observations of longitude north of Panama and only two accurate longitudes for the east coast of North America. Crone notes that the coordinates adopted by Green for those two points, Boston and New York, were remarkably accurate.[17] Green was very forthright about his lack of sources for the interior geography of North America: 'What is inserted of Rivers, Lakes and Nations, to the North and West of the Five Lakes, is in a great Measure Guess-Work; being laid-down from the Report of *Indians*: And as that of Joseph le France seemed to me as credible as any other, I have therefore made-use of it among the rest.'[18] Nevertheless in the west, he took only the small Lake Ouinipique [Winnipeg] and Red Lake, possibly identifiable as the shape of Lake of the Woods and the double lake on the Nelson River system from La France.

The geography of the supposed De Fonte voyage as just mapped and published by Joseph Nicolas Delisle and Philippe Buache in Paris in 1752 and 1753 was commented upon by Green in some detail. The report of the purported voyage of 'Admiral De Fonte' in 1640 from the Pacific Ocean at about 53 degrees north, through passages connecting to Hudson Bay, in effect a northwest passage, had been published in an English journal of 1708. Few paid much attention to it at the time but with the renewed interest in the subject of the Northwest Passage some decades later, several supporters of the theory came forward. Arthur Dobbs, a proponent of the passage theory, published the De Fonte letter in his *Account of Hudson's Bay* (1744). However Dobbs believed (as he showed in the La France map) that the De Fonte voyage in effect was not through the continent but along the coast of North America which trended to the northeast to Baffin Bay.[19] In 1748–9 the first map of the De Fonte voyage, *A Chart for the Better Understanding De Font's Letter*, appeared in Theodore Drage's book on a search for the Northwest Passage from the Hudson Bay side.[20] In 1752 and 1753 J. N. Delisle and Philippe Buache published maps and accounts of the De Fonte voyage[21] which they then attempted to reconcile with the recent Russian discoveries by Bering and others. These maps brought the question of the geography of the west coast to the forefront of contemporary discussion.

Against the background of this controversy about the De Fonte geography, Green had some very astute comments to make in his *Remarks* accompanying the publication of the 1753 *Chart*. He began by stressing that he did not believe in the existence of the De Fonte geography but went on to criticize Delisle and Buache for not even following the account as given and placing their rivers, lakes and passages too far north by 10 degrees. Green indicated that he had received Delisle's map but only when the *Remarks* were being printed did he also receive the accompanying Explanation. In that he noticed that

31

the '5' in 53 degrees north had been changed by hand to '63' to conform with the map. He accused them of doing this to accommodate the De Fonte geography to the Russian discoveries and to allow space for the large Mer de l'Ouest further south. In addition Green pointed out that they showed the termination point of the waterways not in Hudson Bay, as in the original account, but in Baffin Bay which was not only further north but icebound. This, he said, furnished a stronger argument against the possibility of a northwest passage than did the purported De Fonte account. Green added that in a second map which he received just before the memoir went to press they had corrected the locations to the more southerly point of 53 degrees and that Delisle pretended that Buache had not followed his instructions.[22] Further he thought it unlikely that the 'Sea of the West', which they showed near the Pacific Ocean, existed and that its delineation on the map must be the same as the mythical Tahuglak Lake originating from Guillaume Delisle and Lahontan maps at the beginning of the century. Green's *Chart* was finished and published after his memoir. He noted that he had used all of these sources to make his map, while the main part of his notes was written before he received the material from Paris, for which he had included a postscript in the text. Oddly enough, Green also indicated that he would reserve further comment on De Fonte and Delisle's map 'for a Memoir to support a Chart which I have prepared of the Countries round the North Pole: In order to shew the Probability of both a North-East and North-West Passage; either by going round the North Coasts of Asia and America, or els, sailing directly across the Pole itself.'[23] Further speculation about this chart is pointless as it appears never to have been published.

Despite the small scale of his 1753 *Chart of North and South America* (approximately 1 : 20,000,000) Green managed to show a considerable amount of information for the area west of the Great Lakes. He still showed the River of the West emptying into the Pacific at 45 degrees at the opening purportedly discovered by Martin d'Aguilar in 1603 and he retained a large lake north of 55 degrees that is probably meant to be 'Lake Michinipi' or 'Grande Eau' found on some of the La Verendrye maps as well as those by Buache. He showed a very reasonable west coast with such points discovered by Drake as Cape Mendocin and Cape Blanco. North of this he included the two entrances purportedly discovered by D'Aguilar and Juan de Fuca. At about 53 degrees he marked 'Rio del Reyes' the entrance according to De Fonte's journal and above 55 degrees the land discovered by the Russian Captain Chirikov in 1741 who was accompanied by J. N. Delisle.

In the following years, both French and English maps dealing with the De Fonte fantasy began to appear. One of them, a small magazine map, may have been engraved by Jefferys in 1754.[24] A significant map refuting the De Fonte geography was also published in the same year by G.-F. Muller of the St Petersburg Academy of Sciences and a member of one of the Russian expeditions to the Far East. He also showed a more correct version of the Russian discoveries in Asia and North America than that depicted by J. N. Delisle on his maps.[25] Despite the greater detail on the map concerning Asia and the routes of the Russians, Muller unfortunately added an overlong Alaskan peninsula west of Mount St Elias. However he also correctly relocated the North American coast, where the Russians had landed, somewhat further east than Green had done and created a more north-south orientation. The rest of the information on the coast further south and in the interior to Lake Winnipeg and Hudson Bay was taken from the Green-Jefferys *Chart* of 1753 as Muller noted in his later work published in an English edition by Thomas Jefferys in 1761.[26] Muller would have been less interested in the interior information but his coastal delineation was influential for Green.

### THOMAS JEFFERYS'S MAJOR MAPS OF NORTH AMERICA

1755 was an important year in the publishing of maps on North America and it inaugurated a spate of map production in the next few years only equalled by that during the American Revolution.[27] This was triggered by increasing hostilities with the French in North America that would lead to the French-Indian or Seven Years' War in 1756. At least five major maps, mainly of the eastern part of the continent, were issued one of which was John Mitchell's important *Map of the British and French Dominions in North America*. Jefferys himself published his map of Nova Scotia, a version of the D'Anville map of North America, his map of New England and a plan of Chignecto Bay. John Green prepared the *New Map of Nova Scotia and Cape Britain* for Jefferys who issued it in May with an accompanying memoir by Green.[28] Again Green methodically analyzed his mainly French sources accepting or rejecting details as appropriate. Marshall notes that on the whole his coordinates were more precise than those of John Mitchell, and Green did criticize Mitchell in his memoir. Green is also credited with producing *A Map of the Most Inhabited Part of New England* which was issued by Jefferys in November 1755.[29] For both maps, as in his 1753 *Chart*, he listed the main sources on the map and noted that places for which he had latitude or longitude observations were underlined. Longitudes west of London are marked in the upper border of the maps and those west of Ferro on the bottom border.

Jefferys's *Remarks on the French Memorials concerning the Limits of Acadia* came out in the following year with a map showing the English rights in the area and two other small maps. From 1757 to 1760 Jefferys published three or four major maps each year including his *Exact Chart of the River St. Laurence* (1757), a pirated version of the Lewis Evans *General Map of the Middle British Colonies* (1758), plans of Halifax and Quebec in 1759 and the 12-sheet *New Chart of the River St. Laurence* by James Cook (1760). During this fruitful time for his business Jefferys must have been kept busy overseeing the compilation, drafting, engraving and publishing of these maps. Jefferys was clearly given access to many maps held by the Office for Trade and Plantations and from time to time was given permission to engrave and publish maps in their possession,[30] but he had no monopoly on this publishing. Skelton also notes that after the late 1750s Jefferys had a wealth of material in his shop to supplement the Cook charts of the coastal areas, but this would not have been the case for the western part of the continent.[31]

Although mainly preoccupied with the French claims and conflict in eastern North

America, Jefferys clearly retained his interest in the mapping of the western parts of the continent because of the impact on the public of the De Fonte geography and the Russian discoveries. In addition J. N. Bellin had just published a new map of North America (and memoir) showing the La Verendrye explorations west of the Great Lakes and Jefferys or Green or both must have felt this was an opportunity for a new map incorporating these discoveries and essentially showing the connections between the east and west sides of the continent.[32] The resulting manuscript map was published by Jefferys in 1760–2 as *A Map of Canada and the North Part of Louisiana with the Adjacent Countrys* (see figs. 2, 3). The manuscript and the final printed map represent a major attempt to analyze the geography of the interior and west coast not hitherto undertaken by any other English mapmaker (and only a few French ones). Both are important if hitherto unacknowledged contributions to the mapping of the interior and west coast at that time.

## THE MANUSCRIPT MAP OF CANADA AND ITS SOURCES

The anonymous manuscript map, 'A Map of the Northern Parts of America', is preserved in the King's Topographical Collection at the British Library (see Plate III).[33] Nothing further is known about the provenance of the map or when it entered the Royal Collections, prior to their transfer to the British Museum in 1828, and the British Museum's catalogue of manuscript maps of 1844 describes it only as 'A "map of the northern parts of America," between 35° and 60° N. lat.'.[34] It must have remained in Jefferys's possession until possibly 1761 or 1762 when he appears to have finished engraving the plate for the western extension to the printed map. However, it was not listed in an inventory of manuscript and printed maps owned by Thomas Jefferys, made in 1775.[35] As the map is unfinished it was clearly not a presentation copy for the King nor was it a fair drawing for the engraver. The manuscript map may have been presented when the printed map was finally complete, perhaps to honour the coronation of George III in 1761, but there is no dedication to suggest this was so.

Drawn on a scale of about 1:5,000,000, the manuscript map covers the area from 35 degrees to 60 degrees north (from Virginia to the mid-part of Hudson Bay) and from 45 to 125 degrees west of Ferro (or from mid-Nova Scotia to the west coast and the Pacific Ocean). The rivers, coasts and some place-names are in black ink, while names of physical features, enhancements to the western lakes in the interior, Indian tribes, some forts and notes are generally in red. Major place-names such as lakes, forts, and Indian groups are shown in capitals, while other names are in a cursive hand. A green wash has been added along known coast areas and rivers, while a brown wash with some green is used along mountain ranges depicted as molehills. Uncertain parts of the Pacific coast are shown by a dotted line. In the upper left corner there is an exquisitely drawn coloured cartouche surrounding the title (see Plate IV). The rococo frame of shell-work, vines, leaves and a tree-trunk encloses a title somewhat roughly drafted, but in a decorative floral lettering style. On the left side is a beautifully executed drawing of a North

34

American native with considerable red and blue body tattooing and a partly shaved head with a small feathered headdress. He wears a loincloth and moccasins and has an armlet with a fur piece on one arm. The figure leans on a bow, while the right hand holds an arrow. Both the arrow and a finger of the left hand point to the adjacent west coast; a note indicates that it was discovered by Captain Chirikov and J. N. Delisle in 1741, and this gesture may be suggesting the importance of those discoveries. The artist is unknown but the Indian figure is of interest since it is clearly an attempt at an accurate rendition of a native unlike the Europeanized versions of natives in many cartouches on contemporary maps. Although the depiction of the native is apparently not accurate to one tribe or another, it is probably an amalgamation from various eastern tribes and certainly not a western or plains Indian for which there were not yet sources from explorers' accounts. Although further work on the source for this image remains to be done, the figure does bear some resemblance (particularly in the braid of hair and topknot) to engravings of Cherokee chiefs after paintings by Sir Joshua Reynolds which appeared in journals in 1762.[36] The artist probably had easy access to similar sources in London in the late 1750s.

There are several main features to this large map which are important for its period. The geography of the Manitoba lakes (Lakes Winnipeg, Manitoba and Winnipegosis) is of particular importance and this is the first British map to depict them somewhat realistically. The depiction of the west coast is also of great interest. The manuscript map (and the printed map) are certainly oddities in terms of map design for the period since they show only a middle section across the continent; most other general maps at the time included the whole continent, or just its eastern part. But the area shown on this map is the main area put in question by the De Fonte mapping, and the Russian discoveries. On the other hand it is south of the area in Hudson Bay where a northwest passage was being sought. In addition, by depicting a blank area between the central region and the west coast (rather than showing imaginary geography) this map made an important geographical statement in an era prior to extensive exploration. The questions are then, who made this map and the printed map and why and how do they relate to the other Jefferys maps of this area.

While it is possible that an unknown cartographer created the manuscript map and gave it to Jefferys to engrave, it seems more probable, given the close relationship between these two maps, that it was compiled for Jefferys. It also seems likely that John Green was initially responsible for it before his death in 1757. There are several features which point to Green's involvement. First, it is my contention that the map was laid out from the two North America sheets (Sheets III and IV) of Green's *Chart of North and South America* of 1753, which extend from the Equator to 60 degrees north (see fig. 1). The compiler would have been able to create a general layout of the map from the northern halves of those two sheets. Other similarities to Green's earlier *Chart* include the Wright-Mercator projection, which was unusual at the time for maps of continents, and the longitude grid based on Ferro. A longitude grid originating at Ferro had also been used on the Nova Scotia and New England maps, although neither is on the

35

Mercator projection. The choice of the Mercator projection may seem unlikely for Green, who had a wide knowledge of projections, but the area of the map was unusually wide from east to west and narrow from north to south. This was probably the best way to project it, particularly when there were source maps that could be adapted for this purpose. Much of the geography of the western interior and west coast was then modified from careful analysis of other sources. The only element lacking from Green's characteristic mapping style is the underlining of places for which he had latitude or longitude observations.

The area with the most obvious changes from Green's *Chart* of 1753 is the delineation of the rivers and lakes west of Lake Superior and ending with a representation of the lakes in what is now the province of Manitoba. The configuration in this area is based on Bellin's map of North America of 1755 and perhaps other maps by him and on Philippe Buache's *Carte Physique des Terreins les plus elevés de la Partie Occidentale du Canada* (1754).[37] Both Bellin and Buache derived their information from the manuscript maps of the La Verendrye explorations. However, they used different La Verendrye maps as their models.[38]

The main shape and orientation of the Manitoba Lakes on the manuscript 'Map of the Northern Parts of America' would seem to be taken from a mix of the maps by Bellin and Buache. Bellin on his 1755 map shows three lakes in the Manitoba area: Lac Bourbon and south of it Lac Ouinipique and to the west Lac des Prairies. All of the lakes and particularly the latter are shown curved as they were on the La Verendrye source maps and curving incorrectly towards the east; the former two lakes are shown as fairly broad in width. However, the orientation is now generally north to southeast. On the 'Map of the Northern Parts of America' these lakes have been drawn as both wider and uncurved and in slightly more of a north–south orientation. This may have resulted at least partly from plotting the lakes on a Mercator projection whose effect, in contrast to Bellin's conic projection, would be to straighten the lines, widen the shapes and hence make them squarer. This shape is in fact very similar to that on the Bellin world map of 1755 which was on a rectangular projection (see n. 37 below). On the other hand, the compiler has delineated a three-chambered Lake Winnipeg (a possible interpretation of this rather irregularly shaped lake) which must have been derived from Buache's *Carte Physique des Terreins* (1754) as was the main part of the river and lake system from Lake Winnipeg to Lake Superior. Indeed Buache and J. N. Delisle used this version of these lakes and rivers on all of their maps relating to the De Fonte fantasy and added it to their revisions of maps by Guillaume Delisle at this time. The shapes, therefore, would have been available from many printed map sources, but the Bellin map of North America must have been instrumental in determining the orientation. Further north, the 'Lac des Forts' (named only on the printed map) is shown on the Rivière Bourbon [Nelson River] system as depicted on the Buache map, while Bellin shows a similar lake on the Churchill river system. The other river connections north of Lake Bourbon are largely from Bellin. The large unnamed lake at the end of the 'Rapid River' on both Jefferys's maps appears to be the 'Lake Michinipi' or 'Grande Eau' from the Buache map, as this feature was not included on the Bellin map. The 'Mantons River' is from Bellin, and the Assiniboels or Charles River leading to the 'River of the West' follows the shape of Buache. One note here comes from Buache, but the note on the 'Mountains of Bright Stones' is from the Bellin map. Most of the Buache-Delisle maps show the 'Mer de l'Ouest' just beyond the interior geography but Jefferys's compiler has been prudent in omitting this.

It appears, then, that the Jefferys maps are a fairly careful integration of the best information from the two most current sources for the Manitoba area and as such a useful contribution to the cartography of the western interior.[39] Two features on the manuscript map which have not been identified are a western 'Bay Numchibann' on Lake Bourbon and a 'L. d'Esprit' shown west of 100 degrees and just below a note about the Mandan villages. Neither of these appeared on the printed map, suggesting a lack of confidence in their truth, and their origin is not traceable to the Bellin or Buache maps or other contemporary maps.

For the west coast, the map follows the outline of Green's 1753 *Chart* for the southern parts and the Muller *Nouvelle Carte...* of 1754 for the northern coast. A note at 59 degrees North indicating land discovered by Bering in 1741 was also taken from Muller's map. An addition of a dotted line between the openings of De Fuca and D'Aguilar seems to be from the Bellin map of 1755, but Bellin had then tentatively shown a partially inland 'Mer de l'Ouest' which was not included on the Jefferys maps. On the other hand, although Bellin agreed with Green that the De Fonte geography did not exist, he was much more tentative about showing the coast seen by the Russians. He clearly felt that proof that they had seen the coast was lacking, and he included only a few disjointed sections of coastline on his map.[40] On the manuscript map midway along the coast, a note has been added: 'Land which is supposed to be the Fou-Sang of the Chinese Geographers', referring to a publication in 1752 which proposed that the Chinese had made a voyage to North America around A.D. 458, and which had probably first appeared in map form on Buache's *Carte des Nouvelles Découvertes entre la partie Orient^{le}. de l'Asie et l'Occid^{le}, de l'Amérique* in 1753.[41]

On the manuscript map, no 'River of the West' is shown on the west coast, a marked departure from the 1753 *Chart*, the Muller map of 1754, and in a sense from the Bellin map of 1755 in which he had replaced his earlier river of the west concept with the 'Mer de l'Ouest'. Elsewhere on the map a large inland sea with a passage to the south in Labrador is tentatively shown on both the manuscript and printed map but is marked 'Very doubtful'. This is the 'New discovered sea' shown on the 1753 *Chart* and a few other maps of the mid-1750s and which may be from the Dobbs-La France map of 1744.[42] The Bellin map of 1755 had a long note in this region indicating that there was definitely no water communication in that area but rather a long chain of mountains. It is likely that the compiler of Jefferys's maps was influenced by this in designating the water passage as doubtful.

The delineation of the Great Lakes on the manuscript map, and all of the contemporary maps being discussed, differs on every one and is only of interest here in trying to determine which source was used. Malcolm Lewis has provided evidence in an analysis of fourteen maps of the Great Lakes produced between 1745 and 1796 that even in that later period there was no indication of progressive improvement in the areas, shapes or locations of the Great Lakes. Further he has shown that the correlation of shapes in terms of areas common to six of these maps was extremely low, Lake Michigan being least well depicted.[43] It is thus extremely difficult to account for variations in the shapes of the lakes and to come to conclusions on sources used in this period. Lewis indicates that Green's *Chart* – despite the small scale – 'was remarkably good in representing the areas of all but Lake Ontario' and had better representations for shape and location with the exception of Lake Superior which was placed too far to the southwest.[44] However, in the manuscript map which was twice as large in scale the compiler was trying to improve the delineation by consulting hopelessly conflicting sources. The greatest difference between the two maps is Lake Michigan which is oriented more to the southeast/northwest on Green's *Chart*, while on the manuscript map and the printed map of 1760–2, it is oriented southwest/northeast somewhat similar to D'Anville's map of 1755. In general the configuration of the Great Lakes, on both the Jefferys maps, bears the greatest similarity to elements from both the D'Anville maps of 1746 and 1755 (which are different) and is certainly closer to those than the Bellin map of 1755. This was a wise choice since Lewis shows that the D'Anville maps consistently portrayed better shapes and areas for the Great Lakes than the Bellin maps.[45] However there are enough differences to indicate that other sources may also have been used; for instance, both Lakes Superior and Erie have squarer forms than on both the D'Anville maps.[46]

For the rest of the map, it seems clear from the Nova Scotia and Gaspé area included that the compiler used the Jefferys-Green map of Nova Scotia of 1755, although the orientation of part of the St Lawrence differs and seems along with the rest of the coast to be drawn from Bellin's map of North America of 1755. Much of the interior was probably taken from Lewis Evans's *General Map of the Middle British Colonies* which Jefferys had republished in 1758. All of the French and English forts prominent in the Seven Years' War are shown. In terms of establishing a definitive date for the manuscript map, the latest piece of dateable information shown may be Fort William Augustus on the upper St Lawrence River; this was the former French Fort Lévis renamed after it was captured in 1760. This fort, for some reason, was not included on the printed map.

To review the circumstances under which the manuscript map may have been made is somewhat difficult without more external evidence. However, it seems likely that sometime after completing the maps of eastern North America for Jefferys at the end of 1755, John Green started to draft the 'Map of the Northern Parts of America' drawing mainly upon the geography in Bellin's map and memoir of 1755 and the Buache maps of 1753–4.[47] He was very familiar with all of the sources described above and particularly with Bellin's maps. Initially Jefferys's (and possibly Green's) interest may have been in depicting the French discoveries; after all Jefferys's strongest geographical statements were made in the area of the French claims and presence in North America. But Green must also have been interested in refining the western geography of North America from his earlier *Chart*. It is certainly very likely that the map was compiled initially by Green or someone working under his direction since no De Fonte geography is shown. After Green's sudden death in 1757, Jefferys may have left the project for some time but eventually found another compiler/draftsman to add more place-names and perhaps an artist to finish it off with a decorative cartouche. While there are some variations in the use of red or black for names (for instance, in the interior many places and notes are in red, while names and notes on both the east and west coasts are entirely in black) and in the form of some of the lettering, no clear reasons for the differences are evident. Moreover, it seems unlikely that one person commenced the map in black or red and that another person finished it in the other colour. Nevertheless, it is clear from an examination of the printed map that the manuscript map was left unfinished.

### PUBLISHED VERSIONS OF THE MAP OF CANADA

On 2 January 1760 an advertisement appeared in the *Daily Advertiser* (London) indicating that Thomas Jefferys's book, *The Natural and Civil History of the French Dominions in North and South America*, with eighteen maps and plans would be published later that month. And indeed the book was advertised as published on Wednesday 16 January 1760, one day later than promised.[48] The first undated state of the printed version of Jefferys's manuscript map, retitled *A Map of Canada and the North Part of Louisiana*, appeared in this book (fig. 2).[49] The map was a truncated version of the manuscript map extending only to 99 degrees west of Ferro or to include the Manitoba lakes. Since the book was centred on the eastern part of North America and had little if anything to say about the geography west of the Great Lakes, this version seemed to complement the text appropriately. Indeed, Jefferys's use of a different title for the map seems to suggest that he wanted a map specifically to go with the book, not a general map of the northern parts of America but one showing the Canada of the French claims and new discoveries, including the north or west parts of French Louisiana at the rear of the northern English colonies. To emphasize this he extended the map in the east to include all of Nova Scotia and the tip of Newfoundland, but reduced the southern coverage by five degrees to include areas only from Philadelphia north. In general, the map was a fairly faithful copy of the manuscript map although there are enough differences to indicate that the latter was definitely not a fair copy for the engraver. Most of the place-names on the manuscript map were copied onto the printed map but in the eastern part about sixty more names were added. Since the manuscript map was left unfinished, a fair copy with all the additions was probably prepared for the engraver.

*The Natural and Civil History of the French Dominions* received varying responses. Reviewers noted that it was based on Charlevoix's *Histoire et déscription de la Nouvelle France* originally published in 1744, and other French sources. One contemporary described it in the *Critical Review* as an imperfect work but of merit in that the book was made for the maps rather than the other way around. The reviewer was clearly critical

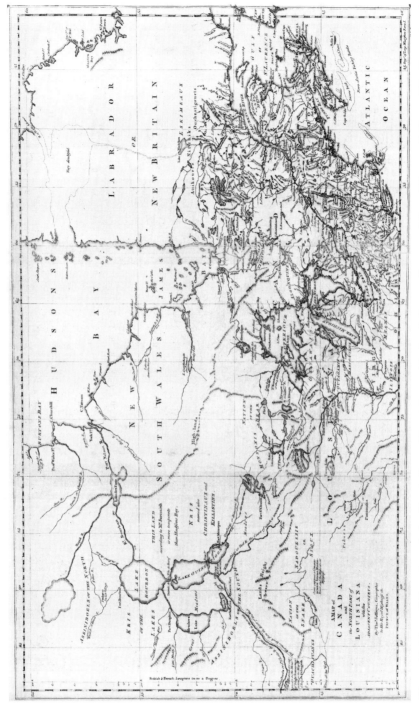

*Fig. 2.* 'A Map of Canada and the North Part of Louisiana with the Adjacent Countrys' from Thomas Jefferys, *The Natural and Civil History of the French Dominions in North and South America*, 1760. BL, 9555.h.3

of the text as simply a translation from imperfect French sources but paradoxically the maps were deemed to be excellent since they were copies from French maps! The *Monthly Review* dismissed the author as clearly lacking literary and critical abilities but praised the maps as particularly well executed, and from the most authentic and current surveys.[50] In fact this was Jefferys's first large gathering of his maps of America, six of which related to Canada, and whether or not reviewers simply thought they were copies of French originals, they were clearly well received. In the text itself there is a short discussion of the area west of the Great Lakes including a full discussion of the French forts in that area for which it is noted the distances between them are taken from Bellin's *Remarques sur la Carte de l'Amerique* (1755).[51] Jefferys's book was reissued in 1761 with the addition of information on the British conquests in America, changes to the title-page and with bibliographical changes to the map. With the accession of George III to the throne in October 1760 and his Coronation in 1761, Jefferys had become Geographer to His Majesty and had changed the author statement on his map accordingly and added a dated imprint. Since the imprint is dated 1762 it is possible that the new issue of the book came out late in the year or in early 1762.[52] The '2' in the imprint is so oddly shaped that it looks as if it were originally 1760. This suggests that there may have been another earlier state with that date although one has not been found. But it is also possible that Jefferys made the changes to that plate in preparation for the extended version of the map which would come out with the translation of Muller's *Voyages* in late 1761 or early 1762 and then found that he wanted to reissue the *Natural and Civil History*. There are, however, no differences in the map. To make matters more complicated one of the copies of the 1760 edition of the book seen by the author has the second state of the map (dated 1762) and a 1761 edition of the book has the earlier undated state of the map. Either these maps were added later to complete copies of the books or there were disbound copies of the books lying around and the maps were carelessly gathered into the different editions.[53]

In late 1761 or more probably early 1762 Jefferys brought out his *Voyages from Asia to America*, a translation of Gerhard Friedrich Muller's accounts of the Russian explorations and discoveries in the Pacific and the west coast of America from volume three of his general history of Russia.[54] The most important map included with this was Jefferys's version of Muller's *A Map of the Discoveries made by the Russians on the Northwest Coast of America*. Jefferys's map is a copy of the original Muller map of 1754 with minor additions made in the second state of 1758 and hence depicts the same interior geography in North America and names on the west coast as drawn from John Green's 1753 *Chart*.[55] However, since Jefferys was simply publishing a translation of a foreign work which had not included maps, he had the freedom to include other maps and an extended version of his *Map of Canada* and two other maps speculating on discoveries in the Pacific Ocean were added. One of the latter was a small map of the De Fonte voyages 'copied according to the Forgeries and pretended Discoveries collected by Messrs. De Lisle and Buache'.[56]

Listed as the third map in the book, the *Map of Canada* was described on the title-page as 'A large Map of Canada, extending to the Pacific Ocean, containing the New Discoveries made by the Russians and the French' (fig. 3). For this map an additional western section was engraved and joined with the eastern part so that the map extends to the west coast as in the manuscript map. The join is at 95 degrees west of Ferro and notes and features beyond this on the smaller version of the map have been copied onto the new plate.[57] The only difference in that part of the map is that the 'River of the West' is shown extending very slightly further west. The west coast is a very close copy of the manuscript map except for the deletion of Lac d'Esprit and the addition of Mount St Elias at the extreme upper left. Despite the transcontinental extension of the final version of the *Map of Canada* to include a careful depiction of the west coast and the Russian discoveries, Jefferys's note in his Editor's preface indicates that he still had the diplomatic problems with the French in eastern North America foremost in his mind. He says that the map will show:

the great Extent the French gave to Canada, even into the very remote Parts of this vast Continent. What End they could purpose to themselves by publishing such Falsities, in regard to the Form and Situation of Part of the Globe, is not easy to determine, unless by a Pretence of having first discovered the whole, they intended to lay Claim to all the Eastern, as well as to drive out and exclude us from all the Western Shores of the Northern Parts of the New World; if so, we have now the Pleasure to see their Artifices meeting a proper Retaliation from an injured Nation, and, instead of gaining by their Encroachments upon others, they have lost all their valuable Settlements, and must in the End, if we preserve what has been gallantly, as well as justly purchased by our Swords, be totally subjugated in North America.[58]

As we know of the existence of the manuscript map, and given his statement in the preface, it is clear then that the enlarged version of the printed map was not created as an afterthought. It would seem that Jefferys had planned all along to issue a full version of the map, despite appending it to a publication to which it did not wholly relate.[59] Why Jefferys did not produce the full version of the map earlier is uncertain since this would seemingly have been easier to do.

One of the most prominent features of the map is the large blank area in the west and the question arises as to why Jefferys did not fill it with the striking cartouche from the manuscript map. On the small version of the map published first, Jefferys necessarily placed the title in the eastern part of the continent, positioning it in a blank area beyond the Mississippi River in the lower left corner of the map. When he added the western extension to the map he either lacked the time or will to change the title. This seems possible since the Muller book may have been published at the same time as the second issue of the *Natural and Civil History of the French Dominions*. The large western area does seem startlingly blank on the printed map – an area that on other maps in this period would normally have a cartouche to hide the compiler's lack of information for the area. A close examination of several different copies of the large state of the map shows that some of the graticule lines drawn across the western area are very faint or even missing, particularly in the upper area where the cartouche would have been placed. This

42

*Fig. 3.* 'A Map of Canada and the North Part of Louisiana ...', from G. F. Muller, *Voyages from Asia to America*, 1761. BL, Cup.401.k.12.(3.)

43

TABLE I. RELATIVE LONGITUDINAL ACCURACY

| Extent of area | Modern Map | Green 1753 Chart | Bellin 1755 | Manuscript Map | Printed Map 1762 |
|---|---|---|---|---|---|
| Gaspé to Great Lakes | 12° 15′ | 13° 20′ | 12° | 13° | 13° |
| Great Lakes (width) | 16° | 20° | 15° 15′ | 14° 15′ | 14° 20′ |
| Great Lakes to Manitoba Lakes | 4° | 15° | 12° 45′ | 13° | 13° |
| Manitoba Lakes (width) | 4° 30′ | 2° 35′ | 8° | 8° 15′ | 8° 10′ |
| Manitoba Lakes to Cape Blanco | 24° | 19° 35′ | 18° 45′ | 20° | 19° 30′ |
| Cape Blanco to Land discov. by Chirikov 1741 | 9° (estimate) | 13° | 12° | 6° | 6° |
| Cape Blanco to Mt St Elias | 17° | – | – | – | 12° 20′ |

suggests that something was erased from the area but no ghost print can be detected on the few copies seen. Perhaps Jefferys lacked any engraver skilled enough to execute the elaborate cartouche from the manuscript map as quickly as needed. There is evidence that the cartouche on the Fry and Jefferson map of Virginia (1753) was drawn by the artist Francis Hayman and engraved by 'Grignon', possibly Charles Grignion or Grignon. Some of his other maps probably had cartouches by the same artist and engraver since there are evident similarities in style among the maps of Nova Scotia (1755), New England (1755) and the Fry and Jefferson map.[60] It seems possible that the cartouche on the manuscript map was drawn by a different artist and Jefferys lacked either the services of a pictorial engraver of equal calibre in 1761 or the desire to pay him.

Table I shows the relative distances in degrees of longitude between points across the continent for various parts of the main maps under discussion in comparison with a modern map on the Mercator projection. In his 1753 *Chart* Green made the eastern half of the continent to the western end of the Great Lakes several degrees too wide. This was no doubt because of the lack of accurate longitude measurements for either the east or west coast as he noted in his *Remarks*. The greatly exaggerated distance between the end of the Great Lakes and the beginning of the lakes in Manitoba on all of the maps reflects the lack of proper longitude observations in the interior and the attempt to fit in the seemingly considerable river and lake systems derived from the maps of La Verendrye. Although Green was not using the La Verendrye mapping on his 1753 Chart, he showed a small Lake Winnipeg and he greatly underestimated the distance from there to the west coast.

On the manuscript map and the printed *Map of Canada* there is a change in measurements because of the new source maps, including the Bellin map of 1755, from which the author was working. The eastern section through to the western extent of the Great Lakes has been reduced and now comes closer to accurate proportions. But the section from the Great Lakes to the Manitoba lakes still remains about nine degrees too wide while the width of the Manitoba lakes has now increased enormously to about four degrees too wide. The measurements on the manuscript and printed maps are also very similar to the 1755 Bellin map. The measurement from the Manitoba lakes to Cape Blanco on the west coast on the manuscript and printed maps is at least 4 degrees too narrow although increased slightly from Green's 1753 map, while the Bellin map lacks over 5 degrees. The longitude distance between Cape Blanco and the point likely seen by Captain Chirikov has been underestimated on the Jefferys maps while the Bellin and Green estimates are too great. Mount St Elias is marked only on the printed map and is almost 5 degrees too far east. In general the printed map and the manuscript map agree fairly closely, which suggests very careful reduction and drafting in preparation for engraving the map. Finally, in comparing the total number of degrees for the width of the whole continent on the printed map to that of the modern map, it is apparent that the compiler overestimated the width of the whole continent by two and a half degrees. Most of the error occurs in the interior, and is perhaps understandable for an area without accurate longitude observations.

## JEFFERYS'S FURTHER IMPACT ON NORTHWESTERN AMERICAN CARTOGRAPHY

After 1762, Jefferys made no new maps of North America (although he engraved and published those by others) and turned his energies to producing county maps of Britain. In 1764 he brought out a new edition of the Muller book with the same maps as in the 1761 edition. After his bankruptcy in late 1766, Jefferys was forced into partnership agreements with Robert Sayer and also with William Faden.[61] In 1768, with financial support from Sayer, he and Jefferys issued *A General Topography of North America and the West Indies*, an enormous collection of a hundred of Jefferys's maps of North America and the West Indies and a fitting monument to his work.[62] Included in this atlas were states of most if not all of the maps relating to North America and the West Indies that he had published in the preceding decade. Besides the three or four general maps, sixteen others were for parts of Canada. The *Chart of North & South America* was included in its third state; *A Map of the Discoveries made by the Russians on the North west Coast of America* was the same as that published in the 1761 and 1764 editions of *Voyages from Asia to America*; and all the other maps from that work were also included without changes. Item eight in the atlas, the *Map of Canada*, was described as 'A Map of Canada with the North Part of Louisiana, New Albion, and the Discoveries made by the Russians and Spaniards on the West Coast of America. Price 2s.'. In this description Jefferys was now emphasizing the west coast and he dropped any reference to the French discoveries, by now probably considered passé.

Jefferys's final contribution to the mapping of northern North America was the maps he produced for Theodore Swaine Drage's *The Great Probability of a Northwest Passage: deduced from Observations on the Letter of Admiral De Fonte...*, a work Jefferys published in 1768.[63] All three maps with the book supported the possibility of a northwest passage. They were described as 'a Copy of an Authentic Spanish map of America, published in 1608', which shows an eastward trending western coastline for North America; 'The Discoveries made in Hudson's Bay, by Capt. Smith, in 1746 and 1747'; and 'A General Map of the Discoveries of Admiral de Fonte' (fig. 4).[64] The author noted in the preface, 'I cannot pass by Mr. Jefferys Care and Exactness in executing the Maps, whose Care

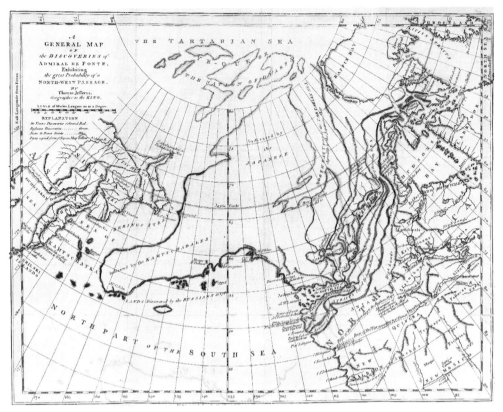

*Fig. 4.* 'A General Map of the Discoveries of Admiral de Fonte' from T. S. Drage, *The Great Probability of a Northwest Passage*, 1768. BL, 569.f.10

and Fidelity to the Publick not to impose any Thing that is spurious, but what he hath an apparent and real Authority for, is perhaps not sufficently known'. It is unlikely that Jefferys as the publisher had any direct influence on the geography as depicted by Drage, however his earlier map production probably influenced Drage in more subtle ways. In his preface, Drage commented further on the maps and tried to reconcile the De Fonte waterways with the purported entrance and passage discovered by Juan de Fuca in 1592 which was usually shown about 47 degrees north.[65] On the De Fonte map Drage used the overly large Alaska peninsula from the Muller map, three 'Rivers of the West' from the Muller map and one location of the 'River of the West' as inferred from the *Map of Canada*. In the interior the Manitoba lakes and rivers have been taken from the *Map of Canada*. The Juan de Fuca strait and passage is shown south of and parallel to the De Fonte passages and both almost connect to Hudson Bay. The Russian discoveries are in place from the Muller map and the *Map of Canada* and the 'Fousang' according to the Chinese has been fitted in between the Juan de Fuca strait and the Archipelago of St

46

Lazarus and Rio de los Reyes of De Fonte. The Tartarian Sea from the Japanese map of the world included in *Voyages from Asia to America* (1761, 1764) runs north-south from the North Pole close to Baffin Bay. Perhaps together, Drage and Jefferys had produced a new and interesting concept of the De Fonte geography mixed with other imaginary geography.[66] While this map was not included in the *General Topography of North America*, Jefferys's earlier map of the De Fonte discoveries copied from Delisle and from the Muller book was included.

The *Map of Canada* seems to have had a short life and perhaps a short influence on other maps. It may not have been sold separately before it was included in the *Natural and Civil History* and the *Voyages from Asia* but it was listed in Jefferys's catalogue of *circa* 1763 with a price of 2 shillings. It was also listed in a catalogue issued by the partnership of Faden and Jefferys in 1774 which took over some of his stock after his bankruptcy and death; but it is not listed in the 1775 manuscript inventory of Jefferys's maps.[67] It is interesting to note that the *Map of Canada* was also omitted from Sayer and Bennett's twenty-three sheet *American Atlas* which included later states of several of the main North American maps by Jefferys and which was first published in 1775 or 1776.[68] However, this atlas was much smaller than the *General Topography of North America* and by then interest had shifted to the English rather than the former French empire in America. Later states of *The Chart of North And South America* and the *Map of the Russian Discoveries* were both included in the Atlas.

The *Map of Canada* was used to update Green's *Chart of North and South America* for the interior and west coast geography in the later state issued by Sayer and Bennett in 1775. But the later states of the Jefferys-Muller map of the Russian discoveries did not show the new interior geography. However, a few other cartographers were influenced by it in making their maps. For instance, Jonathan Carver used part of it for his *New Map of North America, From the Latest Discoveries* (1778) although he preferred the Bellin version of the Manitoba lakes. A few other cartographers such as J. Palairet and Thomas Bowles employed his version of the lakes system on their maps, but on the whole Jefferys's map did not have a large impact on the mapping of North America. The map was important as one of the first reasonably accurate maps and certainly the first British map to connect the eastern and western coasts of the continent. It showed a definite and reasonable western coastline and parts of it were more accurate than Bellin's maps. But in the 1770s both Bellin's and Jefferys's versions of the west were being superseded by maps resulting from real exploration moving inland from Hudson Bay and moving north along the Pacific coast. The map in one sense remained an oddity – a depiction of the continent that neither fully covered the northern half and the Arctic or the southern half and the American colonies. This may have been a reason why it was superseded so quickly in an era that was to see a growing separation between these two areas. On all of his maps of western North America it can be said that Jefferys made an important contribution to the dissemination of both the best information at the time on the Russian discoveries and the French interior explorations, and also to the worst, helping to maintain the concepts of the De Fonte imaginary geography. But his support of sound geographical knowledge in the maps he actually commissioned himself is notable. After his time the only method that would solve the question of the geography of the west coast of America once and for all would be mapping based on real exploration. But the *Map of Canada* though an anomaly remains an important image for Canada – a first concept of the new country that would start to take more definite shape after the American Revolution.

1 The most comprehensive article is J. Brian Harley, 'The Bankruptcy of Thomas Jefferys: An Episode in the Economic History of Eighteenth Century Map-making', *Imago Mundi*, xx (1966), pp. 27–48; see also Coolie Verner, 'The Fry and Jefferson Map', *Imago Mundi*, xxi (1967), pp. 78–80, and Verner and Basil Stuart-Stubbs, *The Northpart of America* (Toronto: Academic Press, 1979), maps 22, 38; Joan Dawson, *The Mapmaker's Eye: Nova Scotia through Early Maps* (Halifax: Nimbus Publishing and the Nova Scotia Museum, 1988); R. A. Skelton and R. V. Tooley, 'The Marine Surveys of James Cook in North America 1758–1768' in R. V. Tooley, *The Mapping of America* (London: Holland Press, 1980), pp. 175–93; several maps are discussed by Douglas Marshall, William P. Cumming and Louis DeVorsey Jr in *North America at the Time of the Revolution: A Collection of Eighteenth Century Maps*, parts ii & iii (Lympne Castle, Kent: Harry Margary, 1974, 1975); William P. Cumming, *British Maps of Colonial America* (Chicago: University Press, 1974); Walter W. Ristow, 'Bibliographical Note' in *The American Atlas 1776* (Amsterdam: Theatrum Orbis Terrarum, 1974).

2 Jefferys's trade card of *c.* 1750 designates himself as 'Thomas Jefferys Engraver' with the title: 'Geographer to His Royal Highness the Prince of Wales...' (BL Maps 187.1.2(18)).

3 Harley, op. cit., pp. 31–3.

4 Apparently Jefferys paid a consideration of £15, an average amount for an engraving apprenticeship at the time. If Jefferys joined Kitchin (who was born in 1719 and apprenticed in 1732) as an apprentice in Bowen's shop in 1735, he must have been born later than 1710 as that would have meant he was starting his apprenticeship at the rather late age of twenty-five. However, there seem to be other possible anomalies with the dates in that Jefferys was also engraving and publishing maps from 1732 and thus before his apprenticeship. Laurence Worms, 'Thomas Kitchin's "Journey of Life", Hydrographer to George III, mapmaker and engraver Part One', *Map Collector*, no. lxii (Spring 1993), pp. 3, 9.

5 Harley, op. cit., p. 30; James Howgego, *Printed Maps of London circa 1553–1850*, 2nd edn. (London: Dawson, 1978), p. 64.

6 *North America*, Thos Jefferys sculp. Several states of this map, some without Jefferys's name, are listed in John R. Sellers and Patricia Molen Van Ee, *Maps and Charts of North America and the West Indies 1750–1789* (Washington, D. C.: Library of Congress, 1981), where this one is item 4.

7 *To his Sacred & most Excellent Majesty George by the Grace of God King...This Map of North America...*, H. Terasson delin. et Fecit (London: Sold by T. Jefferys...& Willm. Herbert at the Golden Globe on London Bridge).; (BL 69915.(81)). Donald Hodson, *County Atlases of the British Isles* (Welwyn, 1984), vol. i, *1704–42*, p. 147, notes that Jefferys probably acquired plates from the Willdey business in 1748 after the death of Thomas Willdey and this is reinforced by two further issues by Jefferys and Herbert of maps originally done by George Willdey: *A new and correct map of the world...*, W. Godson delint (BL Maps CC.2.f.5) and *A new and correct map of the world projected upon the plane of the horizontal...*, C. Price H. Terasson, delin. et sculp. (BL M.T.11.h.2.(17)). The British Library also assigns them dates of *c.* 1750.

8 [John Green], *Explanation for the New Map of Nova Scotia and Cape Britain...* (London: Printed for T. Jefferys..., 1755), after p. 22; Mary Pedley in 'Gentlemen Abroad: Jefferys and Sayer in Paris', *Map Collector*, no. xxxvii (Dec. 1986), pp. 20–3, discusses a selling and perhaps also a buying trip to Paris made by Jefferys and Sayer in 1768.

9 Harley, op. cit., p. 35.

10 For instance, he published and may have written *The Conduct of the French With Regard to Nova Scotia* (1754) and he also published *The Memorials of the English and French Commissaries Concerning the Limits of Nova Scotia or Acadia* (1755). Both of these went into considerable detail about the areas claimed, incorrectly (from the British point of view), by the French on their maps. Ristow, op. cit., p. x, states that the first item was probably written by John Green as it shows considerable familiarity with French maps. See also Harley, op. cit., p. 38.

11 Harley, op. cit., p. 40.

12 Most of the information on John Green comes from the research of G. R. Crone, 'John Green. Notes on a Neglected Eighteeenth Century Geographer and Cartographer', *Imago Mundi*, vi (1949), pp. 85–91; 'Further Notes on Bradock Mead, alias John Green, an Eighteenth Century Cartographer', *Imago Mundi*, viii (1951), pp. 69–70; '"The Retiring Mr Green", In Search of an 18th-Century Cartographer', *Geographical Magazine*, xxv (1952–3), pp. 539–41. The fact that Green was involved in the kidnapping of an heiress in 1728 for which he was lucky to escape imprisonment or hanging probably accounts for his use of an alias, and maintenance of a low profile throughout most of his working life.

13 Crone lists three maps and two texts compiled by John Green for Thomas Jefferys in his 1949 article: *A Chart of North and South America...* and *Remarks in Support of the New Chart...* (both 1753); *A New Map of Nova Scotia and Cape Britain...* and *Explanation for the New Map...* (May 1755); *A Map of the Most Inhabited Part of New England...* (Nov. 1755).

14 Harley, op. cit., p. 40. He also notes that after Green's death he may have had to employ 'an inferior man' which may account for the criticism that his *Natural and Civil History of the French Dominions in...America* (1760) received.

15 J. Green, *Remarks in Support of the New Chart of North and South America; in Six Sheets* (London: Printed for Thomas Jefferys..., 1753). The 'Advertisement' [preface] is dated 20 Dec. 1752 (Canadian Institute for Historical Microreproduction (CIHM) microfiche no. 16764).

16 Green, *Remarks*, pp. 4, 26. This suggests he was consulting J. N. Bellin's *Carte de L'Amérique Septentrionale pour Servir a l'Histoire de la Nouvelle France* (1743) from F. X. Charlevoix, *Histoire et déscription de la Nouvelle France*

(Paris, 1744), which shows the Indian version of river and lake connections, from the La Verendrye explorations, joining up to produce a Rivière de l'Ouest and a Fleuve de l'Ouest ending in the Pacific Ocean. Certainly Green did not use this on his map and he only cites three small scale Bellin maps of the oceans and the world of 1738, 1743 and 1750 for the North America portion. The errors by Bellin for the Great Lakes are borne out by Malcolm Lewis's research, see nn. 43–4 below.

17 Crone, 'John Green', p. 90.

18 Green, *Remarks*, p. 26; the map was *A New Map of Part of North America...the Western Rivers & Lakes falling into Nelson River in Hudson's Bay, as described By Joseph La France a French Canadese Indian who Travaled thro those Countries and Lakes for 3 Years from 1739 to 1742* which was included in Arthur Dobbs, *An Account of the Countries adjoining to Hudson's Bay* (London, 1744).

19 See note above. Much of this is discussed by Glyndwr Williams in *The British Search for the Northwest Passage in the Eighteenth Century* (London: Longmans, 1962), especially ch. 7.

20 The map was 'Drawn by Edward Holding 1748' and appeared in T. Drage's *Account of a Voyage for the Discovery of a North-West Passage... Performed in the Year 1746 and 1747 in the Ship California* (London, 1749), vol. ii, opp. p. 288. See Williams, *The British Search for the North-west passage*, p. 144. But this was a small map with no reference points north of California and an attempt to plot the De Fonte geography only in a general way without reconciling it with known parts of the coastline.

21 Philippe Buache, *Carte des Nouvelles Decouvertes au Nord de la Mer du Sud...Dressées sur les Mémoires de Mr. Del'Isle...* (1750) and J. N. De L'Isle, *Explication de la Carte des Nouvelles Decouvertes au Nord de la Mer du Sud* (Paris, 1752).

22 J. N. Delisle, *Carte Generale des Decouvertes De L'Amiral de Fonte...pour la recherche du Passage a la Mer du Sud* (Paris, 1752) and *Nouvelles Cartes des Decouvertes de l'Amiral de Fonte* (Paris, 1753); Green, *Remarks*, pp. i–iv, 45–8.

23 Green, *Remarks*, p. 48. This seems an unusual theory for Green to have had considering his comments on the ice in Baffin Bay.

24 *A General Map of the Discoveries of Admiral De Fonte & others*, by M De l'Isle. March & Apr.

1754, in *Gentleman's Magazine*, xxiv (April 1754), opp. p. 123. The map appeared with an account mainly of the Russian explorations. Although reference is made to Delisle's map and memorial of April 1750 the map is in fact copied from Delisle's second map dated September 1752. The engraver is not given but could well have been Jefferys, Thomas Kitchin, Emmanuel Bowen or J. Gibson, all of whom were frequently engraving maps for magazines such as these at the time.

25 *Nouvelle Carte des Decouvertes Faites par des Vaisseaux Russes aux Cotes Inconnues de l'Amerique Septentrionale avec les pais adjacents* ... (St Petersbourg: a l'Academie Imperiale des Sciences, 1754 (John Carter Brown Library)). The map was preceded by a memoir *Lettre d'un officier de la Marine Russien* (Berlin, 1753).

26 G. F. Muller, *Voyages from Asia to America* (London: Thomas Jefferys, 1761), p. 74.

27 Malcolm Lewis, for instance, has demonstrated that 28 maps alone showing the Great Lakes were produced in 1755, the highest number for any year between then and the end of the American Revolution: G. Malcolm Lewis, 'Changing National Perspectives and the Mapping of the Great Lakes between 1755 and 1795', *Cartographica*, xvii:3 (Autumn 1980), p. 4.

28 *Explanation for the New map of Nova Scotia and Cape Britain* ... (London: Printed for T. Jefferys ..., 1755). Although Green is not named on the map and in the explanation they are undoubtedly both by him as noted by Crone, 'John Green', p. 90, and also by Marshall in *North America at the Time of the Revolution: A Collection of Eighteenth Century Maps*, part iii, with introductory notes by William P. Cumming and Douglas W. Marshall (Lympne Castle, Kent: Harry Margary, 1975).

29 Crone, 'John Green', p. 91. Cumming notes that Green listed his authorities on the map but did not acknowledge using the important map by William Douglass, which was clearly one of his primary sources, although Jefferys later acknowledged this in the contents of the *General Topography of North America* (1768). William P. Cumming, *British Maps of Colonial America* (Chicago: University Press, 1974), pp. 34, 89–91; *North America at the Time of the Revolution* ..., part ii, with introductory notes by Louis De Vorsey Jr (1974).

30 In the *Journal of the Commissioners for Trade and Plantations* for 1760 it is recorded that their lordships gave Jefferys a small sum and permission to publish a map of Halifax which he had engraved from a manuscript in their possession. Cited in Harley, op. cit., p. 35.

31 R. A. Skelton, *James Cook Surveyor of Newfoundland. Being a Collection of Charts of the coasts of Newfoundland and labradore ... by James Cook and Michael Lane, London, Thomas Jefferys, 1769–70* (San Francisco, 1965), p. 18.

32 Jacques Nicolas Bellin, *Carte de l'Amerique Septentrionale Depuis le 28 Degré de Latitude jusqu'au 72.* (Paris, 1755), accompanied by his *Remarques sur la carte de l'Amerique septentrionale* ... (Paris: De l'Imprimerie de Didot, 1755).

33 'A Map of the Northern Parts of America' (BL King's Topographical Collection CXIX.7–2 – rolled). Manuscript map, drawn in black and red ink, with colour wash along mountains and the coast. Extent: from 35–60 degr. N. and 45–125 degr. west of Ferro. 75 × 147 cm. With a large decorative cartouche in the upper left corner. I am indebted to Edward Dahl of the National Archives of Canada for bringing this map to my attention (National Archives of Canada, photostat copy, microfiche no. NMC 6658).

34 British Museum, *Catalogue of the Manuscript Maps, Charts and Plans ... in the British Museum 1844* (London, 1962), vol. iii, p. 541.

35 'Catalogue of Drawings & Engraved Maps, Charts & Plans the Property of Mr. Thomas Jefferys; Geographer to the King, 1775' (Royal Geographical Society; copy in BL (Maps 203.d.17)); Harley, op. cit., pp. 37, 39, 40, notes that this inventory was probably made in connection with the settlement of his estate.

36 Communication with Dr A. Brownstone, Dept. of Ethnology, Royal Ontario Museum, Toronto. For the Europeanized versions of Indians in cartouches see the maps by John Mitchell and E. Bowen and others reproduced in *North America at the Time of the Revolution*. The engravings of the Indians are reproduced in W. P. Cumming *et al.*, *The Exploration of North America 1630–1776* (New York: G. P. Putnam, 1974), p. 125.

37 Philippe Buache, *Carte Physique des Terreins* ... Publiée sous le Privilege de l'Academie des Sciences, du 4 Septembre 1754. Delahaye l'Aîné Sculpsit. VIIIe Carte in his *Considérations geographiques et physiques sur les nouvelles decouvertes au Nord de la Grande Mer* ... (Paris, 1753–4); Jefferys's compiler may also have

consulted Bellin's *Carte Reduite des Parties Connues du Globe Terrestre* (Paris, 1755). This is on a rectangular projection and shows a very similar shape for the Manitoba lakes to that on Jefferys's maps. However, oddly enough, the lakes are badly oriented to the northeast and placed far too close to Hudson Bay! Bellin might have corrected this for his North America map. The printed map of 1760–2 was described as being derived from the maps of Bellin and La Verendrye but no analysis was made of this in Coolie Verner and Basil Stuart-Stubbs, *The Northpart of America*, map 22, p. 19.

38 The La Verendrye mapping and the various manuscript maps which have survived from his explorations, and were used by Bellin and Buache, are discussed in detail by Richard Ruggles in John Warkentin and R. Ruggles, *Historical Atlas of Manitoba* (Winnipeg: Manitoba Historical Society, 1970), pp. 62–125, and by Arthur J. Ray, 'Early French Mapping of the Western Interior of Canada: a View from Hudson Bay', *Canadian Cartographer*, ix:2 (Dec. 1972), pp. 85–98. Ruggles notes that Bellin took his main shapes for the Manitoba lakes from La Verendrye's 'Carte contenant les nouvelles decouvertes de l'Ouest en Canada' of 1740 (although clearly not the orientation). Philippe Buache on the other hand used a later La Verendrye map as his source, 'Carte des nouvelles decouvertes dans l'ouest du Canada' [post 1750], which shows a three-chambered [Lac Bourbon]- Lake Winnipeg and a two-celled Lac des Prairies and both badly oriented in an almost east-west direction. See Warkentin and Ruggles, pp. 82–5, 110, 118–19, in which all the maps are reproduced; see also Ray, p. 92, for another La Verendrye map with a similar orientation; Conrad Heidenreich in 'Mapping the Great Lakes: the Period of Imperial Rivalries, 1700–1760', *Cartographica*, xviii:3 (1981), pp. 74–109, and esp. pp. 85, 105, also noted that Bellin and Buache were using different La Verendrye maps.

39 Ruggles felt that Jefferys had added 'embellishments of his own devising' and 'has not produced anything significant in Manitoban mapping but presents a configuration already outdated' in his printed map. It is clear, however, that the manuscript map was carefully prepared from current French sources and that both the Bellin and Jefferys maps particularly,

although still a long way from accurate, were the first to show somewhat realistic versions of the shape and orientation of the Manitoba lakes on their printed maps. More accurate maps from exploration would not be forthcoming for another decade; Warkentin and Ruggles, op. cit., p. 122.

40 Bellin, *Remarques sur la Carte de l'Amerique Septentrionale*, pp. 74–5. Bellin's memoir in turn is full of both praise and criticism for Green's *Chart* and *Remarks* of 1753 and at one point he comments 'l'amour de la Patrie n'est pas plus une excuse pour la Géographie'. His thorough discussion of the geography of his map, the improbability of the De Fonte geography and voyage and the problems of plotting the Russian discoveries emphasizes the difficulties all of these cartographers laboured under at this time despite their national points of view.

41 This was Buache's later version of the first map issued by Delisle and himself, and was presented to the Academy of Sciences 9 August 1752 and issued in his *Considérations geographiques et physiques sur les nouvelles decouvertes au Nord de la Grande Mer* (Paris, 1753–4); the report on 'Fousang' was by M. De Guignes and was presented to the Academy in Paris in 1752 and appeared in *Journal des Scavans* (Dec. 1752); Muller, *Voyages from Asia to America* (1761), pp. 74–5.

42 Richard Ruggles, 'Exploration from Hudson Bay' in R. Cole Harris (ed.), *Historical Atlas of Canada* (Toronto: University of Toronto Press, 1987), vol. i, plate 58.

43 G. Malcolm Lewis, 'Changing National Perspectives and the Mapping of the Great Lakes between 1755 and 1795', *Cartographica*, xvii:3 (Autumn 1980), pp. 1–31, and esp. pp. 21–8 and fig. 14.

44 Lewis, op. cit., pp. 22, 24.

45 J. B. Bourguignon d'Anville, *Amerique Septentrionale* (Paris, 1746) and his *Canada, Louisiane et Terres Angloises* (Paris, 1755). D'Anville's 1746 version of the Great Lakes was fairly faithfully copied by Jefferys on *North America From the French of Mr. D'Anville* (London: Thomas Jefferys, 1755) but the compiler of the manuscript and printed maps did not choose to use this delineation of the lakes. See also Lewis, op. cit., p. 24.

46 Tooley shows diagrams of both Jefferys's Lake Huron and Lake Erie suggesting they were

unique perhaps prototype shapes. R. V. Tooley, 'The Mapping of the Great Lakes: A Personal View', in his *The Mapping of America* (London: Holland Press, 1980), pp. 308, 317. However, he has not included the more important D'Anville maps in his group of diagrams. Tooley used only a selection of maps over several centuries and this sort of brief analysis is clearly fraught with problems as Malcolm Lewis suggests in his more detailed study.

47 In 1755, John Green was probably also working on 'A Chart or Map of Europe, Asia, and Africa, improved with Tables and remarks, being a Continuation of the Six Sheet Chart of America' which was advertised for publication at the 'Next Session of Parliament' in his *Explanation for the New Map of Nova Scotia ...* (1755), p. 24; however, this seems not to have been published.

48 *Daily Advertiser* (London), 16 Jan. 1760. 'This Day is publish'd, Elegantly printed in one Volume Folio, dedicated to the Hon. Generals Townshend and Barrington, Price 1 pound 10s. in Boards, illustrated with 18 whole Sheet Maps and Plans and engraved by Thomas Jefferys, Geographer to his Royal Highness the Prince of Wales ...'.

49 *A Map of Canada and the North Part of Louisiana with the Adjacent Countrys.* By Thos. Jefferys, Geographer to His Royal Highness the Prince of Wales. T. Jefferys sculp. in *The Natural and Civil History of the French Dominions in North and South America ...* Illustrated by Maps and Plans of the principal Places, Collected from the best Authorities, and engraved by T. Jefferys, Geographer to his Royal Highness the Prince of Wales (London: Printed for T. Jefferys at Charing Cross, 1760), opp. p. [1] (BL 9555.h.3).

50 *The Critical Review or Annals of Literature*, ix (1760), pp. 47–58; *The Monthly Review or Literary Journal*, xxii (1760), pp. 81–90. Verner and Stuart-Stubbs, *The Northpart of America*, p. 19, mention only that the text is from Charlevoix.

51 *Natural and Civil History of the French Dominions ...* (1760), vol. i, p. 19. This is further proof of the use of the Bellin source as a source for the interior geography on the manuscript and printed maps.

52 *The Natural and Civil History of the French Dominions ... America. With an Historical Detail of the Acquisitions, and Conquests, made by the British Arms in those Parts ...* by T. Jefferys Geographer to His Majesty. (London: Printed

for T. Jefferys ... W. Johnston ... J. Richardson ... and B. Law, 1761) (CIHM 45497); *A Map of Canada ... By Thos. Jefferys, Geographer to His Majesty. 1762. Published by Thos Jefferys near Charing Cross London. (BL Map 70615(16)). Verner in *The Northpart of America*, pp. 252–3, identifies only two states of this map in his bibliography missing the intermediate state.

53 The National Library of Canada holds a copy of the 1760 edition with the second state of the map (CIHM 45494); and the Bibliothèque de la Ville de Montréal has a copy of the 1761 edition with the first state of the map (CIHM 45497). Both the 1760 editions in the Lande Collection, McGill University, and in the Metropolitan Toronto Library have the first states of the map.

54 *Sammlung Russischer Geschichte*, vol. iii (St Petersburg, 1758).

55 'Published by the Royal Academy of Sciences at Petersburg. London. Republished by Thomas Jefferys Geographer to his Majesty.' Verner and Stuart-Stubbs, op. cit., map 38, pp. 272–3; *Voyages from Asia to America, For Completing the Discoveries of the Northwest Coast of America ... serving as an Explanation of a Map of the Russian Discoveries, published by the Academy of Sciences at Petersburgh. Translated from the High Dutch of S.[sic] Muller With the Addition of Three New Maps ... By Thomas Jefferys Geographer to his Majesty (London: Printed for T. Jefferys ..., 1761), p. vii. The note in the Editor's preface states that he has added 'the Routs of the several Travellers by Land and Sea' which would refer to the changes in the 1758 map.

56 *Voyages from Asia to America, ...* (1761), p. viii; *A General Map of the Discoveries of Admiral De Fonte, and other navigators, Spanish, English and Russian, in quest of a Passage to the South Sea*, By Mr. De l'Isle Sep^r. 1752.

57 Most notes have been copied exactly on the second plate; however, the note about the '... Mountains of Bright Stones ...' was moved higher and further to the left and straddles the 100 degree mark. The copy examined in the Thomas Fisher Rare Book Library, University of Toronto (C-10 80) indicates that Jefferys just trimmed the old border off, leaving the former note re 'Bright Stones', engraved the data on the new plate including that note and then pasted it over the edge of the old sheet to join at 95

degrees. However, there is a state of the east sheet in the Library of Congress (Sellers and Molen Van Ee map 95.1, reproduced on microfiche by the Western Association of Map Libraries) showing the east half of the map with the western border and note removed and with the note in the new position but extending beyond the 100 degree mark on the top and bottom borders. Jefferys's engraver might have tried to make the change on the original plate and then realized it was easier to engrave the data from 95 degrees west onto the new plate and join there; this may be a proof copy for this process.

58 *Voyages from Asia to America* (1761), p. viii.

59 *Voyages from Asia to America* (1761) may have been published in early 1762 as it was reviewed in late spring in the *Critical Review*, xiii (May 1762); although the reviewer mentioned Muller's map and one of the others, he did not comment on the *Map of Canada*.

60 Verner, 'The Fry and Jefferson Map', pp. 78–80; *A Map of the Inhabited Part of Virginia* ... Drawn by Joshua Fry & Peter Jefferson in 1751 (London: Thomas Jefferys, [1753]). Verner identified the engraver as Reynolds Grignon who died in 1787, but it may be Charles Grignion or Grignon (1717–1810) who apparently engraved from the work of F. Hayman among others. See Johnson Ball, *Paul and Thomas Sandby* ... (Cheddar, Somerset: Charles Skilton, 1985), pp. 320–1; only Charles Grignon is shown with this variant spelling in the Sidney Lee (ed.), *Dictionary of National Biography*, vol. xxiii (London, 1892), p. 247–8.

61 Harley, op. cit., pp. 42–8.

62 *A General Topography of North America and the West Indies. Being a Collection of All the Maps Charts Plans, and Particular Surveys that have been Published of that Part of the World, Either in Europe or America* (London: for R. Sayer & T. Jefferys, 1768), 4pp. 100 maps on 109 sheets. (BL Maps 12.f.17 (title-sheet and index only); Library of Congress Atlases 1196).

63 Williams, *The British Search for the Northwest Passage*, p. 155, identified the author as probably Capt. Charles Swaine, a seaman familiar with Hudson Bay and hired by Benjamin Franklin to make inquiries in Boston about information in the De Fonte letter. Subsequent research showed that Swaine was really Drage who had accompanied Francis Smith on his 1746–7 expedition to Hudson Bay to look for an opening

for a Northwest Passage. See Howard Eavenson, *Swaine and Drage, a Sequel to Mapmaker and Indian Traders* (Pittsburgh: University of Pittsburgh Press, 1950) and Norah Story, *The Oxford Companion to Canadian History and Literature* (Toronto: Oxford University Press, 1967), p. 223. An inscription on the flyleaf of a copy of the *Great Probability* ... in the British Library (569.f.10) reads 'Presented by the author, Mr. Dragge'.

64 *A General Map of the Discoveries of Admiral de Fonte, Exhibiting the great Probability of a North-West Passage*. By Thomas Jefferys, Geographer to the King. The map indicates that the various discoveries by De Fonte, the Russians, Juan de Fuca and those copied from a Japanese map would be marked in different colours.

65 Drage, *Great Probability*, pp. x, xi.

66 One final map engraved by Jefferys departs almost completely from any of these geographical concepts discussed earlier. *A Map of North & South America with part of Europe, Asia & Africa By the American Traveller*, in Alexander Cluny, *The American Traveller* ... (London, 1769), shows a small Northwest Passage supposed to occur across a narrow land area between Baffin and Hudson Bays and the 'Ice Sea' above the Alaska peninsula. The rest of the interior is shown as a blank. But as with some of Jefferys's smaller maps for books his role in this appears to have been only as an engraver.

67 *Maps, Charts and Plans Published for, and Sold by Thomas Jefferys, Engraver, Geographer to His Majesty, The Corner of St. Martin's Lane, Charing Cross, London.* [c. 1763] (Bodleian Library) reproduced in Ristow, op. cit., p. viii; *A Catalogue of Modern and Correct Maps, Plans and Charts chiefly engraved by the late T. Jefferys* (London: Sold by Faden, and Jefferys, Geographer to the King, at the Corner of St. Martin's Lane, Charing-Cross, January 1774); 'Catalogue ... the Property of Mr. Thomas Jefferys ... 1775'.

68 *The American Atlas: or a geographical description of the whole continent of America: ...* Engraved on forty-nine copper plates by the late Thomas Jefferys (London: Robert Sayer and John Bennett, 1775 [i.e. 1776?]); Walter Ristow, 'Bibliographical Note' in *The American Atlas 1776* (Amsterdam: Theatrum Orbis Terrarum, 1974), pp. v–xi, discusses the question of the date and the choice of only the most pertinent maps

(presumably relating to the American Colonies rather than the French in North America); see also R. A. Gardiner, 'Thomas Jefferys' *American Atlas, 1776*', *Geographical Journal*, cxlii:2 (July 1976), pp. 355–8.

# TWO MANUSCRIPT MAPS OF *NUEVO SANTANDER* IN NORTHERN NEW SPAIN FROM THE EIGHTEENTH CENTURY

DENNIS REINHARTZ

IN the eighteenth century, through the occupation of Texas and Alta California and for a time parts of Louisiana and even the western side of Vancouver Island on Nootka Sound, the Spanish Empire in North America and with it Spain's imperial expansion globally attained its greatest geographical extent.[1] After a brief five-year occupation, the deliberate abandonment of Vancouver Island in 1795, largely as a result of compelling British finesse, initiated the retreat of the Spanish Empire that was soon to be dynamically accelerated by the revolutions and independence of the new Latin American states from Terra del Fuego to northern California and the Pecos and the Red Rivers in 1808–24. Nevertheless, the earlier advance of the frontier of New Spain further to the north and northeast was of particular and lasting importance. The Spanish-Mexican era still accounts for over half of the history of European presence in Texas, Arizona, New Mexico, and California, and its heritage continues to be a vital part of the cultural identity and diversity of the North American Greater Southwest.

Especially in the north, New Spain was a vast, vaguely delineated, underdeveloped and underpopulated region.[2] With the opening up of the extensive Chihuahuan silver mines and under the rational modernization of empire of the new Bourbon dynasty, the eighteenth century was a period of population growth, restructuring, and reform for New Spain, but with the allocation of only relatively meagre resources. In Madrid and Mexico City by the late seventeenth century the colonies along the northern frontier of New Spain had been adjudged as defensive and non-profitable. They consisted of mostly small, isolated settlements, engaged in a basic frontier trade (e.g. buffalo commodities) with each other and the various at least temporarily friendly Amerindian groups present. Given the lack of real new commitments of resources to protect the region against the attacks of unfriendly Amerindians like the Comanche and Apache and the encroachments of Spain's European rivals, France, Great Britain, and Russia, along the northern frontier, Spanish policy was by necessity innovative and also essentially reactive. Consequently, one tribe of Amerindians was often engaged against another, and a course of quiet containment, as exemplified by the founding of the Texas capital of Los Adaes (near present-day Robeline) in 1721 in western Louisiana, was initiated against the

French.[3] The geographer D. W. Meinig's evaluation of Texas and the northeast is applicable to the whole of the northern frontier of New Spain in the 1750s:

... although it might appear from the considerable sprinkling of names and network of trails on some of the maps of its time as a great northeastern advance of Spanish colonization, it was in fact more an area of widespread missionary failures and of a tenuous feeble thrust against the foreign powers in the lower Mississippi, and it had so little substance as to be affronted almost at will by the Comanches on one side and smugglers and filibusters on the other.[4]

As part of the reform process, in the second half of the eighteenth century frequent official tours of inspection of the northern frontier were made. Intended to help maximize the utilization of finite resources and to facilitate administrative reorganization, they yielded extensive reports accompanied by maps which provided valuable data and observations to the distant Spanish policy makers of the 1700s as they now do to historians and other scholars. The results of one such major expedition of approximately 7,600 miles under María Pignatelli Rubí Corbera y San Climent, Marqués de Rubí, in 1766–8 inspired the *Regulations* of 1772, governing *presidios* on the frontier, to replace the apparently outdated *Regulations* of 1729. These earlier *Regulations* were a result of another extensive tour of inspection carried out by Brigadier General Pedro de Rivera y Villalón in 1724–8 and had generally codified an already largely evolved policy.[5]

The new *Regulations* of 1772 offered a somewhat more assertive policy, but also 'traditional European military solutions to uniquely American problems', advocating efficiency over more costly military escalation, offensive warfare against hostile Amerindians when necessary, and a '"cordon of presidios" spaced uniformly across the frontier from the Gulf of California to the Gulf of Mexico'. Rubí's report had recommended a retrenched, more solidified frontier to be established at about the thirtieth parallel to consolidate thoroughly Spain's hold on the area before expanding further to the northwest or the northeast. Regardless of the intentions of the imperial policy makers, both sets of regulations were in reality little known or applied at the scene and followed only when germane or convenient.[6]

Although Texas especially was one of the least populated areas with only 2,510 Spanish inhabitants by 1790,[7] in the second half of the eighteenth century all of the northern provinces had failed in realizing their originally assessed potentials, hence in part calling for the increased number of official inspections of them at this critical juncture on the frontier. On 29 March 1757, the Viceroy and Captain General of New Spain, Agustín de Ahumada y Villalón, Marqués de las Amarillas (d. 1760) ordered José Tienda del Cuervo, Caballero of the Order of Santiago, a captain of Vera Cruz's dragoons and named 'Inspecting Judge', and Agustín López de la Cámara Alta, a lieutenant colonel of royal infantry and engineers, to lead an expedition of inspection of all the settlements of the *Colonia* of *Nuevo Santander*, then still under the command of its founder, Colonel José de Escandón (1700–70).[8] The 'new colony' of Santander was named after the missionary-friar Diego de Santander and his home province and capital city, the ancient northern Spanish seaport in Cantabria so important to the trade with

New Spain. *Nuevo Santander* was in part the forerunner of the modern Mexican state of Tamaulipas and encompassed the lower Rio Grande Valley and the coast of the Gulf of Mexico from Tampico and the Pánuco River in the south and north into Texas and the Nueces River near present-day Corpus Christi. *Nuevo Santander* was established during the War of Jenkins's Ear in 1739–41 (which led into King George's War – the War of the Austrian Succession – of 1740–8) to stop Britain from seizing this vulnerable stretch of underpopulated coast of the Gulf of Mexico. In *Nuevo Santander*, colonists for the first time preceded the military and the Church in settling a new region. Approximately 6,000 colonists initially founded twenty-three towns and missions in 1755. Laredo (reached by the inspecting expedition by 22 July 1757) in Texas became the most important town as a centre of cattle, sheep, and goat ranching and had a population of 708 by 1789.[9] This tour of inspection which 'reconnoitred of 2,393 square leagues' officially began in the village of San Francisco de Güemes on 28 April and ended in mid-October 1757; the clerk-secretaries of the expedition who drafted the final extensive report, entitled *Testimonio de los Autos ... 1757*, of 143 folios, dated 1 February 1758, were Roque Fernández Marcial and a Franciscan, Fray Francisco José de Haro.

This very informative document still exists in the Archivo General de Indias in Seville,[10] but any maps usually accompanying such a report are missing, although this expedition was ordered specifically to map the colony accurately. However, the Bauzá collection in the British Library Department of Manuscripts includes a very large manuscript map on paper of some 125 × 230 cm., entitled *Mapa General Ychnographico de la nueba Colonia Santander* (Add. MS. 17657; Plate V). This map was apparently drafted at least partially by the little known Haro by order of and undoubtedly under the direction of López de la Cámara Alta, who signed and dated it – '*Mexico V de Febrero de 1758. Agustín Lopez de la camara alta*' – in the lower left margin (fig. 1). This large map is in all probability the missing map (or a close copy of it) from the expedition's final report.[11] And a considerably smaller, related manuscript map on vellum of some 28.5 × 39 cm., entitled *Este Mapa comprende todas las billas y lugares de españoles haci como las Missiones de indios y presidios existentes en la Provincia Nuevo Santander ...*, by Haro (*c.* 1770; Plate VI) exists in the collection of the Cartographic History Library at The University of Texas at Arlington.[12] Together, these two maps are very revealing of *Nuevo Santander* and of the northern frontier of New Spain in the second half of the eighteenth century.

The *Mapa General Ychnographico de la nueba Colonia Santander* exemplifies the best Spanish military mapping of the mid-eighteenth century with topography, rivers, and forests shown, as well as roads and settlements. The commander of *Nuevo Santander*, Escandón, was ordered to provide up to date maps and other information to the expedition by the Viceroy. The grid of latitude and longitude on the map and the various construction lines visible in the Gulf of Mexico suggest that the *Mapa General* was a composite compilation from this documentation. The small compass star, located at the bottom centre of the big map in the '*Golfo y Seno Mexicano*', shows that its orientation is slightly (approximately 9°) to the WSW at the top. The coastline, somewhat generally depicted, extends from Tampico in the south past the mouth of the '*Rio Grande Bravo*

57

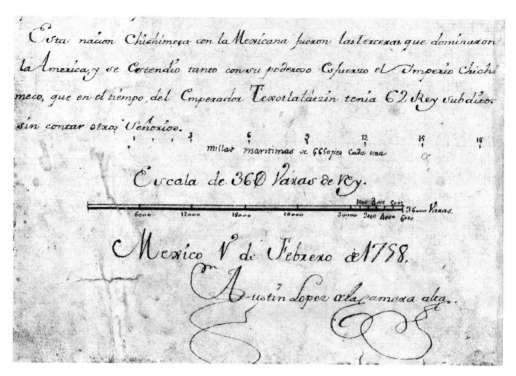

*Fig. 1.* Detail of López de la Cámara Alta's *Mapa General Ychnographico*, showing scales, date, and signature. BL, Add. MS. 17657

*del Norte*' beyond '*Bahia de Sn Miguel*' (the present-day double Nueces-Corpus Christi Bay) to the '*Rio Sn Antonio*' in '*Texas*' in the north. On the eastern side of the exaggerated Rio Grande delta, one of numerous indications on this map of the presence of Amerindians (here perhaps the Karankawas) is made, probably from information supplied by Escandón. While there are extensive indications of coastal wetlands and salt flats ('*salinas*'), there is no indication of the distinctive coastal bending of Texas. The barrier islands like the '*Isla San José*' (present-day Padre Island), the longest such island in the world, stretching some 115 miles from the mouth of the Rio Grande in the south to the Nueces-Corpus Christi Bay in the north, are inexplicably absent.[13] In the Gulf of Mexico, the longitude-latitude grid which covers the entire map becomes clearer and its degrees are indicated, but only Tampico is located by its exact coordinates. Arrays of directional lines also radiate from Tampico and some other major towns in the interior as well as from some important coastal features like the mouth of the Rio Grande. In the map's lower right corner, just above the date and López de la Cámara Alta's signature there are two scales, one in '*Escala de 360 Varas de Rey*' (scale of 360 Royal Rods) and the other, which appears to be a later addition, in '*millas maritimas de 6650 pies cada una*' (maritime miles of 6650 feet each). This corresponds approximately to a scale of one inch to twenty-one miles.

58

Inland, the territory from the coast to '*Guasteca*' and the Sierras '*Madre*' and '*Gorda*' in the south northward to '*Laredo*' and the '*Provincia de Coaguila*' is shown. The towns, villages, missions, fortifications, and roads of *Nuevo Santander* are indicated as are the locations of its various Amerindian populations. In addition to the mountains, hills ('*lomas*'), mesas, passes, plains (e.g. '*Llano de Ramirez*'), deserts (e.g. '*Desierto de 40. leguas*'), wooded areas, and rivers also are scrupulously drawn. The provinces (e.g. '*Jurisdicion de Sn Luis Potosi*') surrounding *Nuevo Santander* are labelled, but none of their features are detailed. The roads are in red, the vegetation in green, and the linework and lettering in black, and the map is shaded grey, perhaps to a large degree the effect of ageing.

Below the title banner across the top of the map is inset a row of small town plans of the Spanish settlements in *Nuevo Santander*, depicting not only each town's layout, but also the surrounding topography. Below each plan is located an often very revealing demographic-economic summary of that settlement in 1757. For example, for the ranching community of Laredo the following entries appear (see fig. 2):

### '*Pueblo de Laredo*'

| | |
|---|---|
| Captain with no salary | 0 |
| Families 12 comprising 84 persons | |
| Working horses | 162 |
| Breeding mares | 701 |
| Breeding cows | 94 |
| Oxen | 4 |
| Mules | 125 |
| Sheep goats | 9080 |
| Male asses | 15 |
| Female asses | 20 |

Somewhat in contrast, for the city of Horcasitas (reached by 24 May) is indicated:

### '*Ciudad de Horcasitas*'

| | |
|---|---|
| Captain with a yearly salary | 500 Pesetas. |
| Sergeant with the yearly salary | 250 Pesetas. |
| Soldiers 9 and each one yearly | 225 Pesetas. |
| Families 73 comprising 367 persons | |
| Indians Bapt. 12 children attached to Mission & others | 95 |
| Clergy with yearly salary | 350 Pesetas. |
| Working horses | 276 |
| Breeding mares | 449 |
| Breeding cattle | 324 |
| Oxen | 68 |
| Mules | 61 |
| Sheep goats | 612 |
| Asses | 3 |

*Fig. 2.* Detail of López de la Cámara Alta's *Mapa General Ychnographico*, showing inset and demographic information for Laredo. BL, Add. MS. 17657

PLATE V

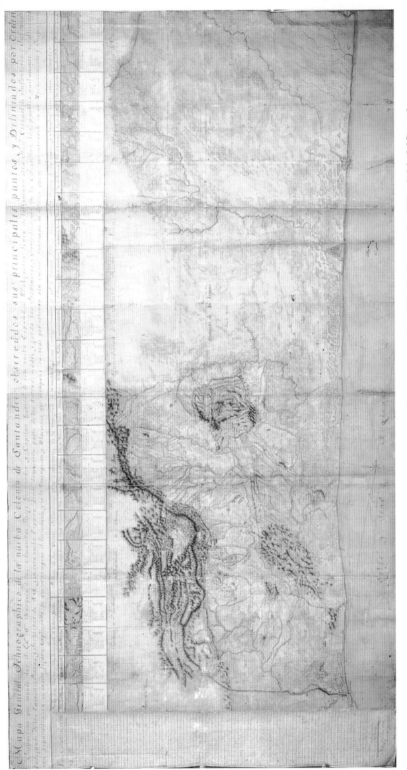

López de la Cámara Alta's *Mapa General Ychnographico de la nueba Colonia Santander.* BL, Add. MS. 17657

PLATE VI

Haro's map of *Nuevo Santander*, with a miniature portrait of its author. *By courtesy of the Cartographic History Library, The University of Texas at Arlington*

This general format is repeated for all the other settlements. Taken in total, these simple statistics help to provide a rare and realistic picture of the province and the daily life of its colonial inhabitants at the time of the inspection.

With regard to the Amerindians, down the right side of the *Mapa general* below the title banner and concluding just above the previously mentioned scales, date, and signature is a lengthy discussion of the '*Vida costumbres i Derivacion de los Indios Chichimecos* (Life customs and Ancestry of the Chichimec Indians)'. Among other things, it is revealed that they are 'dispersed throughout the country', use the fat of various animals to protect their near-naked bodies from the desert sun, and dismember the bodies of respected loved ones among family and friends as relics, preceding an all-night wake. According to the author, the defeat of the 'powerful Mexican and Chichimec Empire' by the 'great Hero Don Fernando Cortes' turned a once gentle people and their descendants into strong, 'knavish' resisters to ongoing Spanish civilizing efforts. And still typical for the times, the origins of the Chichimecs (and other Amerindians) are related to the beginning of the Old Testament and 'the confusion … that occurred 250 years after the Deluge, in conjunction with the Pride of Building the Tower of Babel'. This part of the map provides an informative account of the Chichimecs, synthesizing Spanish observations on their lifestyle and recent history with contemporary Spanish myth-history on Amerindian creation which in turn reflects the long and historic debate on the nature and humanity of these peoples initiated by their first contact with Columbus over three centuries previously.

While it is clearly related to the *Mapa general*, revealing differences in the content and design of the smaller *Mapa* suggest that it was produced at a later date and for a different purpose. The beautifully coloured smaller *Mapa* presents an 'artistic' overview of *Nuevo Santander* in contrast to the detailed, scientific compilation in the larger *Mapa general*. The *Mapa* has no indication of latitude and longitude but is oriented with North at the top. However, the *Mapa* depicts approximately the same area as the *Mapa general* with a similar extent of the coastline along the '*Seno Megicano*' showing the coastal towns, courses and mouths of rivers, great bays, and salt flats in a like manner. And again there are no indications of the distinctive Texas coastal bend or barrier islands. There is no grid, and no consistent scale or scales seem to be operative on this map. A compression and skewing of the geography of this region peculiar to the works of many non-scientific Spanish mapmakers like Haro at this time is present, with for example the Nueces River rightly emptying into the Nueces-Corpus Christi Bay, but just above the mouth of the Rio Grande so that the more than one hundred miles of coastline between the two rivers is barely visible as a wetland.

Inland on the *Mapa* the topographical features are illustrated, and the sites of Spanish habitation are represented by names and differentiated by small building symbols for cities, towns, villages, settlements, and missions. On the entire map, only one non-mission Amerindian habitation site ('*Poblado de Indios*') on the upper reaches of the '*Rio de las Nueces*' is shown. Some of the Spanish sites occurring also signify a later updating of the information on the larger *Mapa general* as evidenced by the smaller *Mapa*

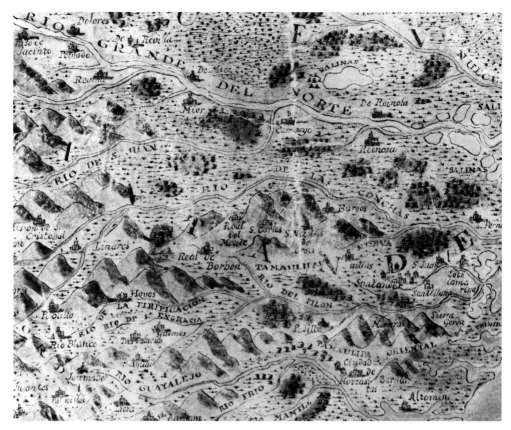

*Fig. 3*. Detail of Haro's map, showing the new settlements of Cruillas, San Carlos, and Villa Croix. *By courtesy of the Cartographic History Library, The University of Texas at Arlington*

recording the villages of Cruillas and San Carlos, founded in 1760, and Villa Croix, founded in 1770, almost at the centre of the map in the mountains just below the bend in the '*Rio de las Conchas*' (fig. 3). The establishing of all three was recommended in the 1758 inspection report to develop further and secure this part of the northern frontier of New Spain. Thus, while it is undated, the smaller Haro map could have been produced no earlier than late 1770.

Across the face of the smaller map, the province, '*NUEVO SANTANDER*', is named in large letters, but between the second '*A*' and '*N*' in '*SANTANDER*', '*Tamaulipas*' also appears. Across the top of the map the title banner also describes the mapped information and names Haro as its surveyor and author. Here the first '*E*' in '*Este*' is sumptuously illuminated in red, blue, and golden yellow. A border in the same style frames the map. Unusually for the late eighteenth century the map has been drawn on vellum rather than paper. Attached to the upper right corner of the map by a red ribbon is a portrait of Haro in the form of a paper medallion (perhaps added later).[14] This black and white intaglio print shows Haro with appropriate symbolism holding a caravel of discovery. The body of the map is also coloured, with the rivers in a light, vibrant blue, the land sand-coloured, and the linework and lettering in black.

Clearly, given its artistry, additions, and date of *c*. 1770, the smaller map was not part of the report of 1758. Unlike the larger *Mapa general*, it is a work of art more than a scientific or official document. The *Mapa* is more an updated recollection of its author than an immediate record. Although very little is known about Haro, the map's elegance and style suggest that he may have intended it as some sort of (commemorative) presentation piece.

The *Regulations* of 1772 called for the appointment of a *comandante inspector*, a commander for the entire military frontier from Alta and Baja California to Texas. The first to hold that post was the Dublin-born Lieutenant Colonel Hugo O'Conor who served from 1772 until 1777. Perhaps Haro's *Mapa* was intended for O'Conor or one of his successors or associates like the French-born Teodoro de Croix, Caballero of the Teutonic Order, who led his own tour of inspection of the area between Durango and San Antonio de Bexar late in 1777.[15] Whatever the case, the *Mapa* in Arlington, Texas wonderfully complements the *Mapa general* in London and continues the story of *Nuevo Santander* so thoroughly told by it.

As well as conveying a picture of a Spanish colonial province in Mexico, both maps betray the European background and attitudes of their makers. The authors of the inspection report, men like Rivera y Villalón, Rubí and Tienda del Cuervo, were still in the eighteenth century hampered by Old World conceptions and vocabulary in discussing New World colonial problems and in formulating possible solutions to them. So, too, were the cartographers of the inspection map like López de la Cámara Alta, Marcial and Haro still using Old World imagery and graphic vocabulary to portray New World geography. Hence, the rolling hills on Haro's smaller map would be more appropriate to areas of his Iberian homeland than to the coastal plains of *Nuevo Santander* in New Spain. Beyond the technology of map compilation, these psychological limitations may also help to explain some of the spatial compression and distortion in their cartographic depictions of the vast landscape of these essentially alien domains. Moreover, it should be remembered that in this latter regard the colonial administrators and policy makers who comprised the principal intended audiences for these reports and their accompanying maps shared in their authors' conceptual limitations, perhaps even more so for being distant from the situations and scenes encountered by the reporters and mapmakers.[16]

Scattered throughout collections in the Greater Southwest, Mexico, the United States and Europe, the numerous maps of inspection of the northern frontier of New Spain in the eighteenth century form an invaluable body of historical resources.[17] They often very beautifully crystallize the political, economic, social, and military situations of the provinces and what Spain really knew (and still refused to reveal) about them and their geographical settings in the late eighteenth century and prior to the Mexican Revolution for independence from Spain of 1810–21. As Meinig again so ably points out, the 'Spanish never had the manpower, skills, or resources' to master the northern frontier of New Spain.[18] Later he continues, 'By the early 1800's the vigor of the expansion was long past and only a thin population of mestizos and Christian Indians along the narrow strip exhibited the Spanish presence...'.[19]

Because of their dispersal these maps and their related reports currently are difficult for scholars to draw upon. As Robert Becker sought out and listed the *diseños* of California ranchos three decades ago,[20] these maps of inspection must be located, catalogued and reproduced to provide more ready access by students of this fascinating time and place. Brought together, as has been done here in only a small way, these inspection maps will then help historians to continue to delineate and re-evaluate this very exciting and formative era in the history of the Greater Southwest and the Spanish Empire in the Americas.

1 At the outset, I particularly want to thank José A. Delgado, my doctoral student and my friend and the Sandra Myres Graduate Research Assistant of the Center for Greater Southwestern Studies and the History of Cartography at The University of Texas at Arlington, for greatly assisting and facilitating my Spanish language translations for this article. I am also indebted to Maritza Arrigunaga, Katherine R. Goodwin, and Shirley R. Rodnitzky from the Division of Special Collections of The University of Texas at Arlington Libraries and to Dr Karen S. Cook, a curator in the Map Library of the British Library, for helping me to secure and understand many of the sources and other materials for this study. This article contains information which was presented previously in a paper, 'Maps from Inspections of the Northern Frontier of New Spain in the Second Half of the Eighteenth Century', at the XV International Congress on the History of Cartography at the Newberry Library in Chicago, 21–25 June 1993.

2 See José Ignacio Echeagaray (ed.), *Cartografía novohispana: una selección de los manuscritos y grabados que, al respecto, se conservan en el Museo Naval de Madrid* (Mexico City, 1980), pp. 11–26.

3 Charles Gibson, *Spain in America* (New York, 1966), pp. 200–1, and David J. Weber, *The Spanish Frontier in North America* (New Haven, 1992), pp. 152, 177–86, and 220.

4 D. W. Meinig, *Imperial Texas: an Interpretive Essay in Cultural Geography* (Austin, 1969), pp. 23–4.

5 Bernard L. Fontana, *Entrada: the Legacy of Spain and Mexico in the United States* (Tucson, 1994), pp. 101–36.

6 Weber, pp. 204–25.

7 Ibid., p. 195.

8 Donald E. Chipman, *Spanish Texas, 1519–1821* (Austin, 1992), p. 169.

9 Weber, p. 194. Also see Herbert Eugene Bolton, 'Tienda De Cuervo's *Ynspeccion* of Laredo, 1757', *Quarterly of the Texas State Historical Association*, vi (Jan. 1903), pp. 187–203, and Lawrence F. Hill, *José de Escandón and the Founding of Nuevo Santander: a Study in Spanish Colonization* (Columbus, 1926).

10 The documents of this expedition also exist published in the *Archivo General y Público de México. Historia*, vols. liii–lvi.

11 *Mapa General Ychnographico de la nueba Colonia Santander observados sus principales puntos y Delineados por Orden è Ynstruccion que mandó dar el Ex^mo S^or Marques de las Amarillas, Virrey Governador y Capitan General de esta nueba España á Dn Agustin Lopez de la Camara alta Tente Colonel de Infanteria é Ingeniero, En Segundo de los Exercitos Plazas y Fronteras de S. M. y en esta nueba España donde demuestra parte de las Sierras madre y gorda las Provincias y Jurisdiciones que la Circundan los pueblos nuebamente establecidos van zeparados con su exacta figura explicando de que se compone el Vecindario, en la que se encontraron en su Reconocimiento é Inspeccion.* [General Descriptive Map of the new Colony Santander showing its principal places and Delineated by the Order and Instructions

that were given by His Excellency the Marqués de las Amarillas, Viceroy and Captain General of this New Spain, to Don Agustín López de la Cámara Alta, Lieutenant Colonel of Infantry and Engineers, on Secondment to the Armies, Fortified Places and Frontiers of His Majesty in this New Spain, wherein it shows parts of the Sierras Madre and Gorda, the Provinces and Jurisdictions that Surround them, the newly established towns are shown separately with exact figures explaining the composition of the Neighbourhood, and in the accompanying Descriptions and Relations all is included without omitting advantages or faults that were found upon Survey and Inspection.], 125 x 230 cm. (Mexico City, 1758), British Library, Add. MS. 17657. It was purchased in 1848 from Francisco Michelena y Rojas, who had bought maps and papers from the widow of Felipe Bauzá y Cañas, former head of the Spanish Hydrographic Office, in 1844. For information on the Bauzá collection, see Peter Barber, '"Riches for the Geography of America and Spain": Felipe Bauzá and his Topographical Collections, 1789–1848', *British Library Journal*, xii (1986), pp. 28–57.

12 Francisco José de Haro, *Este Mapa comprende todas las billas y lugares de españoles haci como las Missiones de indios y presidios existentes en la Provincia de Nuevo Santander para mejor saber de los mismos. Como lo observo y lo dibuxo por orden superior Fray Josep de Aro de la orden de San Francisco.* [This map comprises all the villages and places of the Spaniards as well as the Missions for the Indians and the *presidios* existing in the province of *Nuevo Santander* from the best knowledge about the same. It was surveyed and drawn under the superior orders of Fray José de Haro of the order of Saint Francis.] (Mexico City, *c.* 1770), Cartographic History Library, The University of Texas at Arlington, 86–255, 50/1, X/2. It was purchased from an Austin, Texas, book and documents dealer.

13 King Carlos III made a royal grant of the whole of Padre Island in 1765 to Padre José Ballí after whom it is today named.

14 Also on the *Mapa*, see the third and last volume of Robert Weddle's history of the Gulf of Mexico, *Changing Tides: Twilight and Dawn in the Spanish Sea, 1763–1803* (College Station, 1995), pp. 36–41.

15 See Alfred Barnaby Thomas, *Teodor de Croix and the Northern Frontier of New Spain, 1776–1783* (Norman, 1948 [1941]), and Weber, pp. 220–7.

16 See Dennis Reinhartz, 'New Visions for Old: Encountering New World Imagery before 1800', presented at the Amon Carter Museum, Fort Worth, 15 Feb. 1992, and Eviatar Zerubavel, *Terra Cognita: the Mental Discovery of America* (New Brunswick, N. J., 1992).

17 For example, see José de la Barcanda, *Derrotero hecho para mas conocimiento de las rutas desde Durango hasta San Antonio y desde Chihuahua por el Paso de Sto. Domingo, incluyendo villas, pueblas, presidios, misiones y haciendas…* [A Route Map made for greater knowledge of the roads from Durango to San Antonio and to Chihuahua through the Pass of Santo Domingo, including villages, towns, garrisons, missions and ranches…], 26.5 x 35 cm., sepia ink and watercolour on vellum (Durango: *c.* 1778) in *Catalogue Four* (Austin: Dorothy Sloan Books, n.d.), no. 213 (illustrated), now in the collection of Henry G. Taliaferro of New York City. Stylistically, this map is quite similar to the smaller Haro map. Barcanda was the military Captain of Durango, and according to Jack Jackson of Austin, this map may have been drawn by Luis de Bertucat in part to show the route of Teodoro de Croix's inspection. See also Juan Agustín Morfi, *Derrotero. Hecho por Comandante General Cavallero de Croix* [Route Map. Made for Commanding General Sir Teodoro de Croix], 54 x 56 cm. (Mexico City, 1778), Cartographic History Library, The University of Texas at Arlington, 85–26, 92/1, X5.

18 D. W. Meinig, *Southwest: Three Peoples in Geographical Change* (New York, 1971), p. 12.

19 Ibid., p. 15.

20 See Robert H. Becker, *Diseños of California Ranchos: Maps of Thirty-Seven Land Grants, 1822–1846 from the Records of the United States District Court, San Francisco* (San Francisco, 1964), and Robert H. Becker, *Designs on the Land: Diseños of California Ranchos and Their Makers* (San Francisco, 1969). Similar land-grant documents also exist in Texas (especially those of the Texas General Land Office) and other Southwestern state archives.

# AN EARLY MAP ON SKIN OF THE AREA LATER TO BECOME INDIANA AND ILLINOIS

G. MALCOLM LEWIS

THE British Museum's Department of Ethnography, presently at the Museum of Mankind, London, has on permanent loan a large map made on skin (Plate VII and fig. 2).[1] Centred on the long axis of a diagrammatically straightened Wabash River, when redrawn on a modern map it covers most of what are now the states of Indiana and Illinois (fig. 1). Although occasionally featured in the Museum's own displays or included as a loan item in exhibitions elsewhere, the artefact is little known and has not been an object of serious research.[2] This might at first seem surprising. Maps on skin, though frequently reported from the North American frontier, are rare. Furthermore, this one must have been made and used before 1825, in which year it was brought to England as an ethnographic artefact. There is, however, no immediately obvious intrinsic evidence of its provenance; no title, endorsement, date, personal names, key, or revealing associated document. By tracing the artefact's descent retrochronologically it is possible to establish an intermediate, early nineteenth-century provenance. Thereafter, careful examination of the artefact's physical characteristics and the map's information content has associated them with negotiations with or by Indians prior to a never-implemented major land purchase of approximately fifty years earlier.[3]

## THE ARTEFACT'S LATER DESCENT

The skin is one of sixteen North and South American Indian artefacts now on permanent loan to the British Museum from Stonyhurst College, the Jesuit school that was founded in 1794 near Preston, Lancashire.[4] Most, probably all, were presented to the College in 1825 by Bryan Mullanphy, a pupil from St Louis, Missouri.[5] He had been sent there in 1821 by his father, John, on the second stage of a European schooling that had begun in France in 1818.[6] Boys at Stonyhurst, especially those from overseas, were encouraged to present objects to the College's museum. There is no evidence that young Mullanphy returned to St Louis in 1825, but it is reasonable to suppose that he asked his father to collect and ship Indian artefacts or that the College's appropriate authority asked the elder Mullanphy to do so on his son's behalf.[7] Whether asked to do so by his son or the College, John Mullanphy was ideally placed both socially and geographically to comply. He also had the shipping connections via which to forward the artefacts.[8]

66

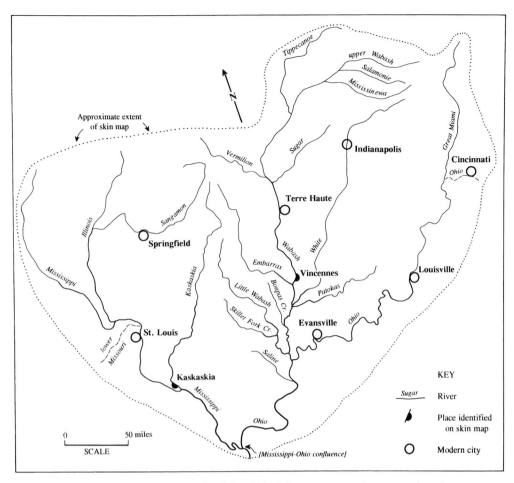

*Fig. 1.* The drainage network of the Skin Map represented on a modern base

John Mullanphy was already a successful entrepreneur when, in 1804, he and his family first came to St Louis by river from Frankfort, Kentucky. Although moving to Natchez, Mississippi Territory, in 1807 and then back to Baltimore, the family returned to St Louis in 1819. An influential citizen during his first period of residence in St Louis, by the time of his return John Mullanphy was a very wealthy man, having made his fortune in the transatlantic cotton trade. In addition, he had invested shrewdly in real estate and was soon to become an equally successful banker.[9] By 1825 he was well placed and financially able to respond to a request for donations to the museum at Stonyhurst College.

By 1825, St Louis had become the hub of the middle Mississippi valley and the gateway to much of the West. It controlled the fur trade in the Missouri valley and the

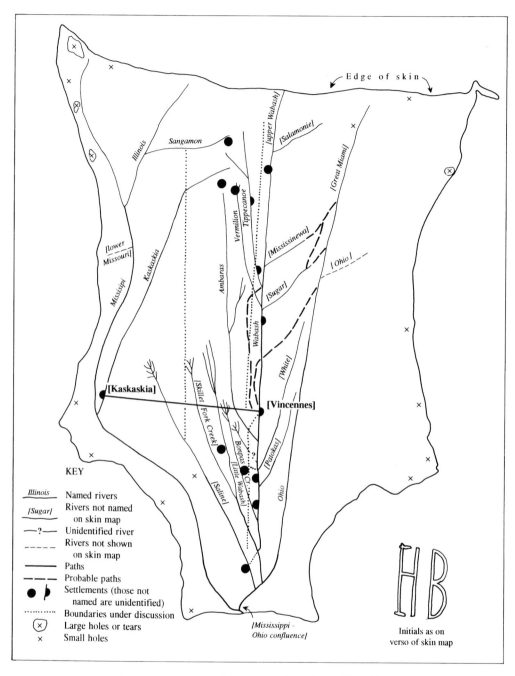

Edge of skin

Illinois

Sangamon

[upper Wabash]

[Salamonie]

[Great Miami]

[lower Missouri]

Kaskaskia

Vermilion

Tippecanoe

[Mississinewa]

[Sugar]

[Ohio]

Ambaras

Mississipi

Wabash

[White]

[Skillet Fork Creek]

**[Kaskaskia]**

**[Vincennes]**

[Patoka]

Bonpas Cr.

[Little Wabash]

[Saline]

?

Ohio

KEY

| | |
|---|---|
| _Illinois_ | Named rivers |
| _[Sugar]_ | Rivers not named on skin map |
| —?— | Unidentified river |
| - - - - - | Rivers not shown on skin map |
| —— | Paths |
| – – – | Probable paths |
| ● ♪ | Settlements (those not named are unidentified) |
| ·········· | Boundaries under discussion |
| ⊗ | Large holes or tears |
| × | Small holes |

[Mississippi - Ohio confluence]

HB

Initials as on verso of skin map

*Fig. 2.* Transcript and interpretation of the Skin Map

68

central Rocky Mountains and was effectively the beginning of the overland trail to the Pueblo communities in the upper Rio Grande valley to the southwest. The self-designated Gateway City of the late twentieth century was already the gateway *de facto*. It was the home of many who in the course of the previous fifty years had been involved in the opening up of the vast, virgin, resource-rich, south-central interior of North America, a region in which Indians were still numerous and, from the alien whites' point of view, either useful and/or exploitable. Exploration, trading, land acquisition and, in the pre-Federal era, international rivalry involving Spain, France, Britain and colonial Americans, involved travelling, living and bargaining with them. Between 1815 and the end of 1820 treaties had been concluded in the city with twelve different Prairie and Plains tribes.[10] Some of its most eminent and wealthy citizens had been involved as commissioners or witnesses in negotiating these and many treaties at places elsewhere in the region, most notably William Clark, Governor of the Missouri Territory and Superintendent of Indian Affairs, and Auguste Chouteau. The co-founder of St Louis, Chouteau was by 1820 the highest taxpayer in the city with $76,000 worth of taxable property.[11] His wealth had been accumulated in the fur trade and related businesses, and his experience with Indians had made him invaluable as a treaty negotiator. In the four years 1815–18 alone, he had been involved in negotiations with twenty-seven tribes and bands.

Mullanphy's connections with Chouteau went back to 1804, when a barge had been sent by 'Messrs. Chouteau' to tow the Mullanphy family's boat up the Mississippi River.[12] More significantly, in or soon after 1819, John Mullanphy had bought from Auguste Chouteau a quarter interest in the land on which the city of Dubuque, Iowa, was later to develop. 'The settlers already on the land and the United States government brought suit against the holders ... and, after a long contest, a decision of the Supreme Court was given against the Chouteau-Mullanphy claim.'[13] Quite clearly, the two men must have had frequent business contacts in the years immediately preceding the Mullanphys' Stonyhurst gift. Whether John Mullanphy had social or business contacts with William Clark, undoubtedly the most important administrator in the city, is not clear. Clark, however, could well have been another source of Indian artefacts. The co-leader ten years before of the famous transcontinental expedition with which his name has ever since been associated, Clark had in 1816, while Governor of the Territory of Missouri, 'established the first museum west of the Mississippi in a fine brick wing to his residence on North Main Street.'[14]

The cultural origins of the Mullanphy-Stonyhurst artefacts are appropriate to a collection made in St Louis: perhaps from the immediate region, a 'Cradle used by Indians of the Mississippi'; from the northeast Plains, a Sioux shield; from the Southwest, two Pueblo shields, probably brought overland via the Santa Fe Trail; perhaps from the Plains, six arm bands made from horn; and four calumets (tobacco pipes) which, though almost universal within what is now the conterminous United States, were particularly characteristic of the northern Plains, source of the catlinite (red pipe stone) from which the best bowls were made. In the context of the North American artefacts in the collection,[15] the skin map is the exception in at least two respects: probably the only one to have originated to the east of the Mississippi River, and westernized to the extent of incorporating written information. Determining its earlier provenance must begin with a careful examination of its intrinsic characteristics.

There is nothing about the artefact or its map that can be dated with certainty. It is, however, possible to determine with reasonable accuracy both the interval of time during which it was made and the focal area with which it was concerned.

The pattern of rivers and unnamed settlements on the skin are of no use in determining dates (figs. 1 and 2). An extensive search in the Geography and Map Division of the Library of Congress failed to discover printed or manuscript maps having even approximately similar patterns of drainage for the region between the lower Ohio and middle Mississippi Rivers. The drainage pattern as represented on the skin is certainly not in either the colonial or federal traditions for the region. Conversely, it has all the hallmarks of being Indian in origin. Primacy is given to the Wabash River. Represented as essentially straight, it is aligned along the spinal axis of the skin like the prime rib of a leaf. The Ohio and Mississippi Rivers frame it to the right and left. Rather than being arranged approximately at right angles to each other, they are presented as essentially parallel. The Mississippi is closer to its edge of the skin and is effectively shaped by it in much the same way as the Arkansas River on the much better known Chickasaw map of *circa* 1723.[16] The relationship of the tributaries to the Wabash River is also typically Indian: essentially straight and joining the main river at acute angles in a manner very similar to that in which tributaries are represented as joining the Missouri and upper Mississippi Rivers on a well known Iowa Indian map of 1837.[17]

The Indian origin of the drainage pattern as represented on the map is supported by two other categories of information: the tribal names *Piankishwa* (appears three times), *Kaskaskias* (certainly appears once and possibly twice), and *Wia* (appears twice);[18] and unexplained circle and semicircle symbols in red, most if not all of which seem to represent Indian villages.[19] The word *Sold* follows the tribal name *Piankishwa* in one instance. None of the symbols is named. Most are placed on one side of a river (all the semicircles) and some on both sides of a river (most of the circles), but a few of the circles are placed away from rivers, and one of these differs from the others in having a dot at its centre. None of the symbols is differentiated in such a way as to indicate white forts or civil settlements, even though there were French forts within the area of the map between 1680 and 1760, British ones from 1760 to 1778, and an increasing number of American civil settlements thereafter.[20] Failure to differentiate any of these does not, of course, exclude the possibility that some of the symbols might have been placed at the sites of white settlements, around virtually all of which there would have been clusters of Indians.

Not only is the geometry of the drainage system centred about the axis of the *Wabach*

70

River, most of the map's information is located within its basin: all but one of the thirteen settlement symbols, three of the five tribal names, and several diagnostically significant essentially straight dotted lines. One continuous straight line links the *Wabach* to the *Missisipi*. Conversely, the peripherally positioned *Ohio* and *Missisipi* valleys are virtually devoid of detail. All this seems to indicate that the map was made in connection with negotiations relating to Indians in the *Wabach* valley and particularly its western part, where more *Wabach* tributaries are shown, as well as twelve of the thirteen settlement symbols, and all the dotted lines.

On the basis of map content it is possible to determine the period during which the artefact was made. It certainly postdates the early eighteenth century. The *Kaskaskias*, named on the map to the east of the *Missisipi* and south of the lower *Kaskaskia*, migrated into that region in 1703.[21] The *Wia*, named in two places on the map on the upper *Wabach*, were reported at Fort Ouiatenon in that general region by 1717.[22] Likewise, the *Piankishwa*, named to the east (where they had already *Sold* land) and west of the middle *Wabach*, were reported near Vincennes in 1720.[23] There seems little doubt that the map could not have been made much before the last date. Establishing its terminal date is much more difficult, because the eventual disappearance of the three named tribal groups from the areas in which they are named on the map involved intra-regional movements, partial outward migrations, and demographic decline. The *Piankishwa* were not completely out of the *Wabach* valley until 1816 and the *Wia* not until 1827.[24] Although by 1796 there were only eight or ten adult *Kaskaskias* to the east of the *Missisipi*, they had inherited a vast territory in the general region in which their name appears on the map[25] and this was not to be ceded to the United States until 1803.[26] General ethnohistorical evidence, therefore, does no more than date the map as having been made sometime between the early eighteenth and early nineteenth centuries.[27]

The only other elements on the map that might help establish a date are several differentiated, approximately straight but unexplained lines. A black, unbroken and perfectly straight line connects a settlement on the east bank of the middle *Wabach* just above its confluence with the *Ambaras* ( = Embarrass River) with another settlement on the west bank of the lower *Kaskaskia* only a short distance above its confluence with the *Missisipi*. The most likely referents for these are, on the *Wabach*, Fort Sackville, occupied by the British from 1769 to 1778 and then by the Americans renamed as Fort Patrick Henry until 1788 and, on the *Kaskaskia*, Fort Gage, occupied by the British from 1772 to 1778.[28] Connecting them on the map by a straight line would be a typically Indian way of representing a military road between them.[29] This tentative interpretation, if correct, would date the map far more precisely than the general ethnohistorical evidence to sometime in the lifespan of Fort Gage: between 1772 and 1778.

The other lines on the map are dotted, and in different colours, some in red and others in black. One, in red, is straight, just to the west of and parallel with the equally straight *Wabach R.* above inferred Fort Sackville. A second line, also in red, is likewise straight. Drawn parallel to but far to the west of the first, it very approximately conforms to the primary watershed between the *Wabach-Ohio* drainage system to the east and the *Kaskaskia-Missisipi* system to the west. The positioning of these two lines suggests boundaries rather than linkages. In particular, there are no settlement symbols along them or at their termini. As no such boundaries are known to have been agreed in the 1770s, it is reasonable to assume that they were drawn in the course of negotiations for land sales to private companies or for inconclusive attempts to make land cessions to the federal government. As Britain's presence in the region before 1778 was tenuous, and the United States Government did not begin to negotiate treaties there until the Treaty of Greenville in 1795, the likelihood is that the map was made in connection with land-sale negotiations involving large areas, perhaps leading to agreements but never implemented. Two such agreements were reached within the period 1772–8 and they were closely related: the Illinois Land Company's purchase from Kaskaskia, Peoria and Cahokia Indians on 5 July 1773 at the town of Kaskaskias, of two parcels of land to the east of the Mississippi River; and the Wabash Land Company's purchase from the Piankashaw nation on 18 October 1775 at Post St Vincent (Vincennes) and Vermilion of two parcels of land on the Wabash River.[30] Although never taken up, all four parcels of land were within the area of the skin map and the purchases were made within the tentatively determined period during which the map was probably made. Clearly, there is a hypothesis to be tested: that the skin map was made by, in part by, or for Indians in connection with negotiations prior to one or both of the agreements to sell land to the Illinois and Wabash Land Companies. Given the concentration of information on the map within the Wabash valley, the latter is by far the more likely.

THE CONTEXT IN WHICH THE MAP WAS MADE AND USED

As early as the spring of 1773 William Murray, an agent for the Philadelphia merchants Michael and Bernard Gratz, was in possession of an edited and abbreviated version of a legal opinion given in London sixteen years before. The original of 1757 had had nothing to do with North America. The Attorney-General, Charles Pratt, and Solicitor-General, Charles Yorke, each in turn later Lord Chancellor, 'had delivered a commentary on the rights of the East India Company for the guidance of the Privy Council in reply to a petition of the corporation ... it represented a specific answer to a question respecting India which the petitioners had raised.'[31] Their opinion read as follows:

As to the latter part of the prayer of the petition relative to the holding or retaining Fortresses or Districts already acquired or to be acquired by Treaty, Grant or Conquest, We beg leave to point out some distinctions upon it. In respect to such Places as have been or shall be acquired by treaty or Grant from the Mogul or any of the Indian Princes or Governments[,] Your Majestys Letters Patent are not necessary, the property of the soil vesting in the Company by the Indian Grants subject only to your Majestys Right of Sovereignty over the Settlements as English Settlements & over the Inhabitants as English Subjects who carry with them your Majestys Laws wherever they form Colonies & receive your Majestys protection by virtue of your Royal Charters, In respect to such places as have lately been acquired or shall hereafter be acquired by Conquest the property as well as the Dominion vests in your Majesty by Virtue of your known Prerogative & consequently the Company can only derive a right to them through your Majestys Grant.[32]

The opinion drew a clear distinction between areas conquered by the Crown and those acquired from native persons or governments. In the former, property was deemed to be vested in the Crown; in the latter, with the company making the acquisition. The version that had come into 'Murray's possession carried a heading denoting that it was the opinion of the late Lord Chancellor Camden and Lord Chancellor Yorke (actually Morden) on "Titles delivered by the King's Subjects from the Indians or Natives," and bore the further notation that the document was "a true Copy compared in London the 1st April 1772."[33] This version read as follows:

In respect to such places as have been or shall be acquired by Treaty or Grant from any of the Indian Princes or Governments; Your Majesty's Letters Patents are not necessary, *the property of the soil vesting in the Grantees by the Indian Grants*; Subject Only to your Majesty's Right of Sovereignty over the Settlements and over the Inhabitants as English Subjects *who carry with them your Majesty's Laws wherever they form Colonys* and receive your Majesty's Protection by Virtue of your Royal Charters.[34]

Notwithstanding the claim that it was 'a true Copy', the version of the opinion in Murray's possession eliminated references to India and the East India Company. By retaining the references to 'Indian Princes or Governments' and to 'Indian Grants', however, it created the impression of pertaining to English lands in North America. This, presumably, was a deliberate deceit. There were also serious omissions. Murray's version of the opinion failed to note the distinction between lands ceded to the Crown by foreign powers (in the case of the Wabash valley, France by the Treaty of Paris, 1763) and those that the Crown had reserved for the use of Amerindians by the Proclamation of 1763. The latter extended from the Appalachian Mountains to the Mississippi River and included all of the area represented on the skin map. Furthermore, Murray's version failed to take into account that, whereas in India the East India Company's charter endowed it with quasi-governmental powers, its nearest North American equivalent, the Hudson's Bay Company, governed territory far to the north and had no authority over the potentially rich lands between the Appalachians and the Mississippi.

The history of the Murray version of the Camden-Yorke Opinion is long and complex.[35] After the Revolution many American lawyers concurred with it, but eventually the contrary view prevailed. Titles to lands acquired from Indian tribes were declared void when the state had not given consent. In the case of the Illinois and Wabash Land Companies a final memorial to the United States House of Representatives was rejected in 1811.[36]

The edited and abbreviated version of the Camden-Yorke Opinion encouraged late colonial land speculators to risk capital and make purchases of land from Indians. Among

73

these, the Illinois Company was the most important. Organized in 1773, its members included William Murray, some Philadelphia merchants, and several Pennsylvania traders. Murray had first gone west in 1768 when he set up in business at Fort de Chartres on the east bank of the Mississippi just above its confluence with the Kaskaskia River. From the outset his activities were threefold: provisioning the British garrison, trading with Indians and land speculation.[37] During the next five years he became very familiar with the region between the Mississippi and Wabash Rivers: its Indians, resources and potential; changing British attitudes and military activities there; the activities of other traders; and the opinions and concerns of the small but growing ethnically mixed civilian population.

In the spring of 1773, Murray returned to the Illinois country with the backing of the Illinois Company and in possession of the edited and abbreviated version of the Camden-Yorke Opinion. He failed, however, to persuade Captain Hugh Lord, the British commander at Fort Gage,[38] that the Opinion was valid. Lord was apparently powerless to forbid purchases of land from the local Indians but warned Murray that he would not allow settlement on lands thus acquired.[39] Nevertheless, after nearly one month of negotiating, an agreement was reached with the Kaskaskia, Peoria and Cahokia, constituent tribes of the Illinois. Two vast tracts of land to the east of the Mississippi were acquired at a total cost later estimated at $37,326.17.[40]

Almost immediately after the purchase the grantees faced opposition from the British authorities. Unable to gain the support of their own colony, Pennsylvania, they sought the sanction of Virginia which, by her charter, claimed the whole of the Northwest, including the Illinois country. On 19 April 1774, Murray, acting on behalf of the Company, presented a petition to the Earl of Dunmore, Governor of Virginia, asking that 'Virginia extend her laws and jurisdictions over their purchase, since it was within her limits'.[41] Dunmore did intercede on behalf of the Company. Although this was ultimately unsuccessful, Murray had almost immediately initiated a second land-purchasing venture that, if successful, would have compensated Dunmore for his intercession. It was almost certainly in the course of this venture that the skin map was made.

In September 1774, Murray started negotiating to purchase lands from Indians on behalf of the newly formed Wabash Company. This time, however, the negotiations were with chiefs and leaders of the Piankashaw for lands in the Wabash valley. Significantly, John, fourth Earl of Dunmore, was second among the unalphabetically arranged list of grantees included in the deed of purchase, dated 18 October 1775. Whereas in the previous year's deed William Murray as negotiator had been listed first, Louis Viviat now appeared first for the same reason.[42]

Why, when Murray had initiated the idea, Viviat emerged as negotiator is not clear. As traders at or near Kaskaskia, the two men would certainly have known each other for several years. Viviat may have been deemed to have had better credentials than Murray. Already well established as a French trader at Ste Geneviève in 1765, by the mid 1770s he was a member of the Kaskaskia gentry, pro-British in the growing tension between

Britain and the American colonies, and must have had considerable understanding of both Indian and white attitudes within the wider region.[43] Viviat's pro-Britishness might have been calculated to maximize the chance of a purchase being acceptable to His Majesty's Government. It must have been hoped his experience of people and extensive network of contacts would advance the negotiating process. Furthermore, his status as a gentleman would have ensured respect. There may, however, have been an overriding political reason for entrusting the negotiations to Viviat. Murray was well aware that French residents in the Mississippi and Wabash valleys had purchased lands from Indians before the Proclamation of 1763. Viviat was one of these. As Anna Marks has written, 'Was the idea that Frenchmen who [had] once bought land from the Indians could do so again...? Did [Murray] reason that the English Crown would not dare oppose such a prominent Frenchman as Louis Viviat who was merely reiterating the acts of other French settlers – on a larger scale of course? By using him, Murray could of course gain the good will of the French.'[44] Indeed, this strategy may in part have led to the selection of the Wabash valley as the region in which purchases were to be negotiated. There had been French military and civilian settlements therein for several decades before the military withdrew in 1760, and in 1773 the region continued to be French in language and culture.

Very little is known about the negotiating process for either the Illinois or Wabash purchases other than can be inferred from the deeds.[45] The two were very similar. That for the Wabash purchases consisted of:

1. The English or French names of eleven 'chiefs of the different tribes' of the Piankashaw who had been involved in the negotiations;
2. The name of the Company's negotiator – Louis Viviat;
3. Mentions of 'different conferences, as well public as others...' and 'treaties and talks we have had together...';
4. The name of the place at which agreement was reached – Post Vincennes;
5. A list of goods to be given to the Indians in exchange for lands specified in 7;
6. The name, status, and place of residence of each of nineteen members of the Company;
7. A word description of the boundaries of two tracts of land being sold by the Indians to the Company;
8. The totem marks of eleven Indian chiefs and one war chief, these being the signatories on behalf of the Piankashaw;
9. The signatures of ten witnesses, all with French family names;
10. A certification by the commandant at Post Vincennes that the two named Indian interpreters had faithfully interpreted between the chiefs and Viviat; and
11. A certification by a notary public that he had faithfully translated into French the original deed written in English.

Of the above, 3, 7 and 10 are significant in understanding the negotiating process. In linking the skin map to that process there is also important evidence in 9.

Thirteen months elapsed between William Murray beginning discussions with the

Piankashaw in September 1774 and Louis Viviat reaching agreement in the deed of 18 October 1775. There must have been many meetings conducted during that period. Likewise, in obtaining the agreement of so many Piankashaw Indians, the negotiations must have been complex.[46] Most difficult must have been reaching and confirming agreement concerning the boundaries of the two 'extend[s] or quantities of lands' to be sold/purchased (7 *supra*). The deed uses almost 400 words to describe the nodal points (named settlements and the confluences of named rivers), lines (named river courses and lines parallel to named rivers or between nodal points) and distances (in leagues between nodal or less well defined points). The negotiations must have been conducted at different levels, some with Viviat but others between Indians, with or without the assistance of advisers and interpreters.

The commandant's certification of the two interpreters (10 *supra*) contains the following statement:

having been duly sworn, [they] have deposed, that they served as interpreters to the savage nations, during all the time they have been in conference, held in the town and village of Post Vincennes and Vermillion, by Louis Viviatte, for himself, as also in the names of different other persons, with the chiefs of the different tribes of the savage nation of Pianguichias, relatively to the purchase of lands, as above mentioned, specified and written in the aforesaid act, which the said witnesses, or interpreters, have faithfully interpreted between the said Louis Viviatte and the chiefs denominated in the aforesaid act; and that the said witnesses, in their quality as interpreters, have done for the best in their souls and consciences, according to the best of their understanding and knowledge, and have, faithfully and plainly, explained to the said chiefs denominated in the aforesaid act, to which they have set their ordinary marks, with their own hands, whereof the signification has been mentioned, and for their consideration, has been explained; as, also, the names of the acquirers; and that the said interpreters should be present at the delivery of the said considerations specified in the act aforementioned; as, also, that they should be present at the passing of the aforementioned act, in the presence of the said chiefs, which have put their marks at the foot of the said act.[47]

From this it would seem that the two interpreters had acted for the Piankashaw chiefs in their formal negotiations with Viviat, in making sure that they were fully cognizant of the deed in the form in which it was ultimately signed by both. They were also to be present at the signing and at the 'delivery' of the goods to be given to the Indians as the purchase price of the land. There is no suggestion that the two interpreters were involved in less formal discussions between the chiefs themselves in the absence of either Viviat or an agent. Neither is there any indication as to the process whereby the boundaries of the two land purchases were negotiated and defined. Evidently it had been a prolonged and complex process, perhaps involving French settlers, who had already purchased smaller lots of land from the Indians, and certainly taking into account the interests of the several scattered Piankashaw villages. There must have been many informal meetings between interested parties from within the region. It is not even known whether, after Murray's first initiative, the Piankashaw offered to sell specific lands or the Company's

PLATE VII

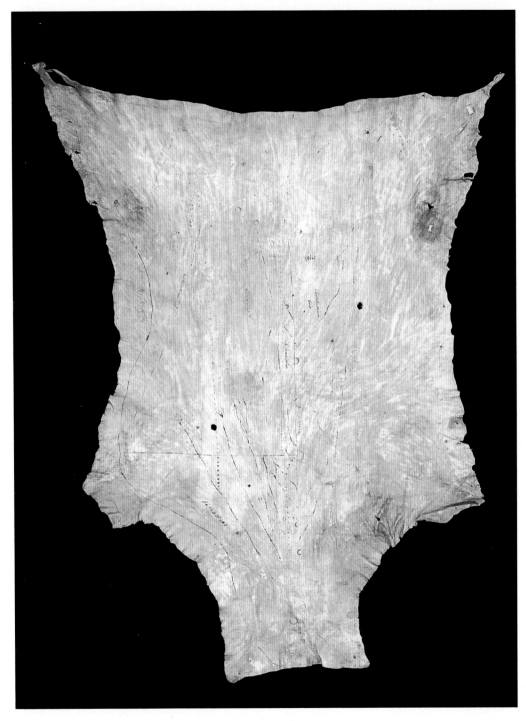

Skin Map of the Wabash River area. BM, Dept. of Ethnography, AM loan 1.3, Stonyhurst 1825.16. *By courtesy of the Trustees of the British Museum*

PLATE VIII

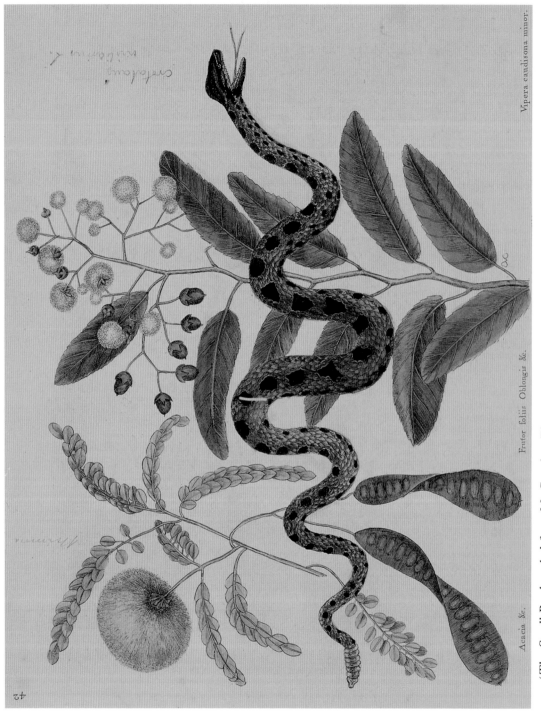

'The Small Rattlesnake' from M. Catesby, *The Natural History of Carolina...*, 1731–43, vol. ii, pl. 42. BL, C.113.i.1

agents (Murray himself or Viviat) sought to purchase specific tracts. Whichever was the case there must have been a complex sequence of boundary defining and redefining. The Piankashaw chiefs would presumably have known the terrain and hydrography very well; some of the French residents fairly well; and Murray and Viviat less well, though they must have had local advisers.

Of the ten witnesses (9 *supra*) and two interpreters (10 *supra*), probably all were members of French families living in the Wabash valley. Identifying them more precisely is difficult. Names were inconsistently recorded at that period and, of the ten witnesses, six did not record their Christian names. Among the latter, the surname Bolon appears eighth in the unalphabetical list. In 1725, a Gabriel Bolon had married at Fort St Joseph.[48] His son, Hypolite François Beaulon (on other occasions spelled Bolon) was baptized there on 31 January 1740.[49] By the early 1760s both father and son were living at or near Post Vincennes. On 18 September 1772 'Baullon' signed a memorial from the inhabitants of Vincennes to General Thomas Gage, as did 'ipolite bolon fils'.[50] Between 1777 and 1806 there are numerous references to Hypolite Bolon being an Indian interpreter.[51] In the absence of either a Christian name or initial, it is impossible to determine with certainty whether father or son witnessed the Wabash Company's deed of purchase in October 1775. One piece of indirect evidence, however, suggests that it was the son. On the verso of the skin map are large initials that presumably indicate personal ownership or possession at some stage in its history. Apparently as old as the map itself, they would appear to be 'HB' (see fig. 2).[52]

Having been born close to the then main Miami village near St Joseph thirty-five years before, Hypolite Bolon would have been well qualified to converse with the Piankashaw. Although independent tribes, the Miami, Wea (*Wia*) and Piankashaw spoke the same Central Algonquian dialect.[53] The Bolon family may even have moved south from St Joseph during the period when the three tribes were doing likewise: the Miami to the upper Wabash valley; another group identifying themselves as Wea to the middle Wabash and the Piankashaw still further south to the Vermilion and lower Wabash valleys.[54] By 1775 Hypolite Bolon had probably achieved little more than local status in and around Vincennes, but thereafter he is referred to in different and wider social and geographical contexts. He moved to New Madrid on the west bank of the Mississippi in the 1780s or early 1790s, where he acted as an Indian interpreter for the Spanish authorities, and ultimately to St Louis, where he apparently worked in a similar capacity for the Indian Department of the United States War Department.[55] He may, however, have been poorly educated or even illiterate. In negotiations for the 1804 treaty between the United States and the united tribes of the Sauk and Fox Indians, 'Hypolite Bolen' was one of the sworn interpreters but on the treaty document his name was last among those of the witnesses and followed by 'his mark', in contrast to the signatures of all the others.[56] Notwithstanding long intervals during which nothing is known of him, Hypolite Bolon's post-1775 activities complement his earlier life in suggesting that he could have had something to do with the making of the skin map by, with, or for the Piankashaw.

The skin map embraces the areas in which the Illinois and Wabash land purchases were negotiated and the intervening area, but not much more. For the Wabash valley, the mapped boundaries are not those defined in the deed of purchase of October 1775. The boundaries do, however, have a common general characteristic. In both the deed and map they are defined in relation to the Wabash River: areas to the east and/or west thereof for stipulated (in leagues in the deed) or constant (on the map) distances between specified (in the deed) or represented (on the map) points. Of the two, the deed is the more precise. It contains sufficient information for the boundaries of the purchased lands to have been surveyed on the ground, though there is no evidence that they ever were. In contrast, because the map does not conserve linear scale and represents the quite complex course of the more than 400 mile-long Wabash River as essentially straight, it was not an implementable document. Nevertheless, the deed and the map contain sufficient information in common to reveal two important differences in information content. The deed includes within the lands purchased two enormous tracts to the east of the Wabash River, whereas the map indicates no boundaries in that direction.[57] Conversely, to the west of the Wabash, the map indicates parallel to the river a dotted boundary that, with one minor deviation near Post Vincennes (marked with a semicircle, unnamed but virtually certain), extends nearly the whole of its length. In contrast, the deed explicitly excludes from the sale an area centred on Post Vincennes, some twenty-four leagues wide on both sides of the river, this to be 'reserved for the inhabitants of' the post. The map also appears to differentiate between the straight dotted boundary line to the west of the Wabash River and north of Vincennes and that to the west and south. The former is certainly red, but the latter is apparently black.

One further element on the map is noteworthy in this context, *Piankishwa Sold*, positioned to the east of the middle Wabash River. No attempt is made to indicate the extent of the area involved, when the sale was made or to whom. If it was a much earlier sale, then no record of it would appear to have survived. Although small lots of land had undoubtedly been sold to French settlers in the immediate region of Post Vincennes, the position on the map is too far north for *Piankishwa Sold* to have referred to these.

SOME INTERIM CONCLUSIONS CONCERNING THE SKIN MAP

On the basis of the above analysis of the skin map and discussion of the historical context in which it was made, it is now possible to evaluate the hypothesis stated on p. 72 that it: was made by, in part by, or for Indians in connection with negotiations prior to one or both of the agreements to sell land to the Illinois and Wabash Land Companies. The following conclusions are not equally certain, but this is inevitable when so much of the context involved unrecorded frontier activities by persons now unknown or little known. It is, therefore, useful to assess subjectively each conclusion as virtually certain (vc), probable (pr) or possible (po). They are as follows:

1. The extant skin map, or an earlier state of it, was made after the Illinois Land Company's deed of purchase dated 5 July 1773 for lands to the east of the

Mississippi River[58] but before the Wabash Land Company's deed of purchase dated 18 October 1775 (vc);

2.  The geometry and graphical content of the extant map indicate that it would have been intelligible to Indians and was made according to their traditions (vc);

3.  The extant map has such finely executed linework and excellent calligraphy that it may have been a contemporary augmented copy of a cruder original (pr);[59]

4.  At some stage the extant map belonged to or was in the possession of Hypolite Bolon (vc);

5.  The map was made and used in the course of the thirteen months of negotiations prior to the Wabash Land Company's purchase of land from the Piankashaw Indians (vc);

6.  The map was not necessarily used in direct negotiations between Louis Viviat, on behalf of the Wabash Land Company, and representatives of the Piankashaw. It could have been an interim document made and used in discussions between different sub groups of the Piankashaw (pr), between the Piankashaw and French land owners in and around Post Vincennes (pr) or between the latter and Louis Viviat (po);

7.  The use of a red dotted line for the northwest boundary and a black dotted line for that to the southwest might indicate that negotiations were being conducted with at least two subgroups of Piankashaws (po);

8.  The map may have been made after the Piankashaw had agreed in principle to sell land to the northeast of Post Vincennes (po)[60] but in the course of negotiations to exclude from sale lands across the river from that Post that had already been sold to and settled by the French (pr);[61]

9.  The extant map was at some stage displayed vertically (vc) and may have been used as a group discussion document (pr);[62]

10. If the extant map functioned as an interim discussion document, its contextual value would have been shortlived (pr) and it would not necessarily have been seen by all the final signatories and witnesses to the deed of purchase (po).

### THE ARTEFACT'S PROBABLE EARLIER DESCENT

In all probability the skin map, made in 1774 or 1775 for a locally important but short-lived purpose in or near Post Vincennes, was found in or before 1825 approximately 150 miles to the west in St Louis. When it was made, St Louis was a small, ten-year old and ethnically mainly French village in Spanish territory, the economic, demographic, and cultural links of which were down the Mississippi. Incorporated in 1808, five years after it had become United States territory under the terms of the Louisiana Purchase, St Louis then grew very rapidly, partly as a focus for ethnically French migrants from within the region and partly as a centre of opportunity as perceived by entrepreneurs from the eastern States. It seems highly probable that the skin map reached St Louis via one of these migration routes, the former far more likely than the latter.

It is possible, but relatively unlikely, that Bryan Mullanphy's father, John, could have brought the map to St Louis in 1804 after living in Philadelphia and Baltimore from 1792 to 1798 and in Frankfort, Kentucky, between 1798 and 1804.[63] The first two places had been the home regions of more than half of the original members of the Wabash Land Company. That, however, was seventeen years before the Mullanphys arrived from Ireland. Furthermore, it is difficult to imagine why an interim document (6 *supra*) should have passed into the hands of any of the sleeping partners, none of whom had even been present at Post Vincennes to witness the 1775 purchase. At Frankfort, the Mullanphys were much closer to St Louis and Vincennes and, through the family's well developed Roman Catholic connections, were in contact with the region's older French families.[64] The skin map could conceivably have come into John Mullanphy's possession via one of those contacts, but it is difficult to imagine what significance the artefact would have had for a man with a keen sense of the present and an entrepreneur's attitude towards the future. The arguments against John Mullanphy having himself obtained the skin map in the east apply with equal or greater force to other St Louis inhabitants from the middle Atlantic states. A French cultural connection, through either Louis Viviat or Hypolite Bolon, would seem much more likely.

If the skin map was deposited as evidence during the final negotiations for the Wabash land purchase, this could account for its surprisingly fine linework and calligraphy (3 *supra*). The most likely recipient would then have been Louis Viviat, and he could have brought it to the central Mississippi valley. He died in Kaskaskia less than three years later, when his affairs were dealt with by his attorney, John Gabriel Cerré.[65] By then Cerré had lived in the Illinois region for more than twenty years and become an authority on its history, laws and customs. Indeed, in 1786 he was consulted by a committee of the United States Congress on matters pertaining to Illinois, including several aspects of land law.[66] If the skin map was in Viviat's possession at the time of his death in 1778 Cerré would certainly have appreciated it and could well have taken it to St Louis when he moved his home there soon after purchasing a plot of land in 1779.[67] Between then and his death in St Louis in 1805 he became 'the patriarch of a considerable portion of the [presumably French] inhabitants of the settlement' and exerted 'a great influence in the management of its affairs'.[68] Items in his possession are likely to have passed to others, most probably fellow residents of St Louis, before or at his death. The recipient of the map may have given it at a later date to John Mullanphy, who had first arrived in that still small community in the year before Cerré died. This hypothesis, or a variant of it, is certainly more probable than the suggestion, considered earlier, that John Mullanphy could have brought the artefact to St Louis from the east.

Another and still more likely possibility is that Hypolite Bolon brought the skin map to the middle Missouri valley; perhaps even to St Louis itself.[69] Because of his apparent inability to sign his own name in 1804, it is very unlikely that he made the calligraphically excellent extant map. He could, however, have obtained it either in the course of negotiating with Piankashaw Indians on behalf of the French land owners in and near Post Vincennes (6 and 8 *supra*) or in assisting a subgroup of the Piankashaw in negotiations with one or more other subgroups (6, 7 and 8 *supra*). As a man of relatively low status in early nineteenth-century St Louis, he may not have mixed socially with the ranks of local society, but his work certainly brought him into contact with them. As an interpreter for the Sauk-Fox treaty of 1804, he was one of only eleven non-Indians.[70] The most senior of these was William Henry Harrison, Governor of Indiana Territory and the District of Louisiana. Pierre Chouteau senior, a member of the St Louis-based fur trading family, was a member of the same negotiating team. He was also the person who two years later listed 'H. Bolon' as one of the employees of the 'Indian Department'.[71] This was one of the 'Messrs. Chouteau' whose barge had towed John Mullanphy's boat up the Missouri River in 1804.[72] Furthermore, it was his brother, Auguste Chouteau, with whom in 1819 John Mullanphy jointly invested in land.[73] If Bolon brought the skin map to St Louis, as seems probable, it may well have passed to John Mullanphy via the Chouteaus.

### THE SIGNIFICANCE OF THE SKIN MAP

The artefact is significant in three respects: as a rare example of an Amerindian (or Amerindian-influenced) map on skin; as evidence that maps were at least occasionally used in negotiations leading to land sales and land cessions by Amerindians to whites; and as a source of otherwise unknown information concerning settlements in the Wabash valley in 1774–5.

Indians in many parts of America are known to have made and used maps on skin. The earliest reported example dates from 1540, when Francisco Vásquez de Coronado found a 'skin' (probably buffalo robe) with a 'painting' or 'sketch' on it of the seven Zuñi pueblos and of the route that would appear to have linked them.[74] In 1793, Thomas Jefferson's instructions to André Michaux, concerning the latter's proposal for an expedition from the Missouri River to the Pacific coast, advised that:

The method of preserving your observation is left to yourself according to the means which shall be in your power. It is only suggested that noting them on the skin might be best for such as may be the most important, and that further details may be committed to the bark of the paper birch, a substance which may not excite suspicion among the Indians, and little liable to injury from wet or other common accidents. By the means of the same substance you may perhaps find opportunities, from time to time of communicating to the [American Philosophical] society information of your progress, and of the particulars you shall have noted.[75]

Although Jefferson, influenced no doubt by his eastern woodlands perspective, recognized skin and birchbark as the typical media of the Indians, extant maps thereon are rare. Hence, even though it may well have white components such as words, the Stonyhurst skin map is a rare extant example of a once fairly common and geographically widespread form of indigenous cartography.

Very few Indian-white land-sale deeds or cession treaties were accompanied by maps. Furthermore, there are very few detailed accounts of negotiations prior to sales and treaty agreements. A rare example describes how, on 2 August 1805, a Mississauga Indian, negotiating with the British to sell land west of Toronto 'spoke with a flat stone in his hand on which was represented the lines within which they had on a reconsideration agreed to give their Father [George III]'.[76] The 'reconsideration' had been hasty and the map had been scratched on the stone in the twenty-four hours since the previous meeting. The account is of a map made to facilitate negotiations already in progress. Occasionally, Indians made maps to initiate sales as when, on 16 November 1770, an Indian informed George Washington about land suitable for farming in the upper part of the Buffalo (now Bull) Creek valley south of the Ohio River in what is now Washington County, Pennsylvania. Washington was on a private expedition with the intention of purchasing potentially rich agricultural land. The Indian, who was possibly a Mingo, brought to his attention land he had not seen and would not see, chalking 'out upon his Deer Skin' [perhaps cloak] the situation of 'a fine piece of Land and beautiful place for a House'.[77] These are glimpses of map-based Indian-white interaction, once perhaps fairly common, on and ahead of the frontier of white settlement. The Stonyhurst skin map is a rare surviving example, though whether used as an initiating or negotiating map is not clear.

Because this artefact has been shown to date from 1774 or 1775, it is also a potential source of information about the pattern of settlement in the Wabash valley at that point in time. Seven red circles and seven semicircles undoubtedly represent settlements, two of which can be identified with certainty: Kaskaskia and Post Vincennes. Although semicircles and circles appear to distinguish between settlements sited on one side of a river and settlements sited astride or away from rivers, there is no obvious explanation for differences in radii. None are named and the topological structure of the base data (river patterns) together with an absence of distinctive detail (e.g. river meanders) preclude the identification of precise ground sites. Even so, there are more settlements on the map than indicated in secondary sources. Most are probably Indian and their distribution *vis-à-vis* each other merits analysis in relation to the best of these sources. In this context, Helen Hornbeck Tanner's *Atlas of Great Lakes Indian History* is the obvious starting point.[78]

After more than two hundred years, during most of which it has been virtually unknown, the Stonyhurst skin map has at last been dated and placed in its geographical and historical context. Scientific physical analysis and detailed archival research would doubtless modify some of the above conclusions. It is unlikely, however, that such work would lessen in any way the historical value of the artefact as an example of an Indian or Indian-style map made in the course of Indian-white negotiations concerning land.

This paper is based on research conducted over a period of more than ten years, during which many individuals have provided advice and information. Of these, the following merit special thanks: Father M. Bossy and R. G. Mitchell of Stonyhurst College, for information about Bryan Mullanphy and his gift of Indian artefacts; Karen S. Cook of the British Library Map Library, for producing the finished line maps; Richard Day of the Lewis Historical Library, Vincennes University, for invaluable information about Hypolite Bolon; Jonathan C. H. King and his staff at the Museum of Mankind, for answering many questions and arranging for the author to make two examinations of the skin map; Margaret W. Pearce of Clark University, for volunteering to conduct biographical research in Chicago; and Charles H. Perkins and friends for delightful hospitality in St Louis.

1 British Museum, Dept of Ethnography, AM 1977 loan, 1.3, Stonyhurst 1825.16. Dimensions 137 × 91 cm. Untitled map of the Wabash valley and adjacent parts of the Ohio and Mississippi valleys. Black and red (ink or dye) linework and names on (deer?) skin. Undated and without title, endorsement, or scale. The verso has the initials HB. These letters lack ink or dye but are etched into the skin; probably as a consequence of corrosion arising from the chemical decomposition of the pigments with which the initials were originally applied. The Stonyhurst College museum register describes the artefact incorrectly as follows: 'Map of Arkansas River and its tributaries on hide'. How this gross error arose is a matter for inconclusive speculation.

2 The artefact's existence was first publicized in the catalogue for a major loan exhibition: J. C. H. King, *Thunderbird and Lightning: Indian Life in Northeastern North America 1600–1900* (London, 1982), fig. 89, pp. 84 and 95. More recently it was reproduced in the catalogue for an exhibition at the University of Essex: Pauline Antrobus *et al.* (eds.), *Mapping the Americas* (Colchester, 1992), p. 63. Neither catalogue gives much information about the artefact or offers a significant explanation of the map's origin and purpose.

3 Although sometimes creating grammatical dilemmas for the author, it has been found helpful to distinguish between the artefact as a physical object and the map thereon as a source of information.

4 British Museum, Dept of Ethnography, Stonyhurst 1825.16, .18, .19, .20, .21, .22, .23, .24, .26, .27, .28, .30, .31, .32, .33 and .39. There is a distinct possibility that related items may have been lost. On occasions the College's museum was reputedly raided for stage properties.

5 Except where indicated otherwise, all biographical information concerning Bryan Mullanphy is from the biographical entry on him in William Hyde and Howard L. Conard (eds.), *Encyclo-pedia of the History of St. Louis* (New York, Louisville and St Louis, 1899), vol. iii, pp. 1585–6, or from the entry on the Mullanphy Emigrant Fund on pp. 1586–91 in the same volume. Unfortunately, the Mullanphy Family Papers, 1780–1951, in the Missouri Historical Society, St Louis, include very few pre-1825 items.

6 Except where indicated otherwise, all biographical information concerning John Mullanphy is also from Hyde and Conard (eds.), op. cit., pp. 1591–3.

7 Correspondence between several members of the family during the period Oct. 1825-Feb. 1827 suggests a degree of estrangement between Bryan and his father, apparently arising from the son's wish to leave Stonyhurst College: Mullanphy Family Papers, Missouri Historical Society. It is possible, therefore, that Bryan may not have been well disposed towards the College. On the other hand his father John would have been receptive to requests from educational institutions, especially when they were Roman Catholic foundations. The brief biographical statement compiled by the archivist and enclosed with the Mullanphy Family Papers states that John was the 'first Anglo-Irish merchant in St. Louis, and St. Louis's first millionaire ... He brought to St. Louis three religious orders of women and established their convents. Possessed the best library west of the Mississippi.' His concern for education was such that, in addition to educating Bryan in France and England, he eventually sent each of his seven daughters to Ursuline Convents in either Rouen or Lyons: Hyde and Conard (eds.), op. cit., p. 1592.

8 From 1792 to 1798, John Mullanphy lived in Philadelphia and Baltimore, two ports having major maritime connections with England. Before moving to St Louis he had fitted out a schooner and engaged in the West Indies trade. In 1815, at the end of the War of 1812, he had sold a large consignment of New Orleans cotton in Liverpool: Hyde and Conard, op. cit. Bryan's fees at Stonyhurst College were paid through a Liverpool firm: letter to the author dated 10 June 1983 from R. G. Mitchell, Head of Geography, Stonyhurst College.

9 John Mullanphy's business activities during this period are summarized in Alice Lida Cochran, 'The Saga of an Irish Immigrant Family: the Descendants of John Mullanphy', Dissertation

Presented to the Faculty of the Graduate School of Saint Louis University in Partial Fulfillment of the Requirements of the Degree of Doctor of Philosophy, June 1958, pp. 54–9.

10 Kansa (1815); Sauk of Rock River, Winnebago, and Ottawa with Chippewa and Potawatomi (1816); Menomini (1817); Quapaw and Osage (1818); and Kickapoo (1820). Charles J. Kappler (comp. and ed.), *Indian Treaties 1778–1883* (Mattituk, New York, 1972), pp. 123–4, 126–8, 130–1, 132–3, 138, 160–1, 167–8, 189–90.

11 Cochran, op. cit., p. 60.

12 Hyde and Conard, op. cit., pp. 1591–2.

13 Ibid., p. 1592.

14 John C. Ewers (ed.), *Indian Art in Pipestone: George Catlin's Portfolio in the British Museum* (Washington, D. C., 1979), n. 2, p. 34.

15 One of the artefacts is from outside North America: 1825.18, South American Mantle.

16 'A Map Describing the Situation of the several Nations of Indians between South Carolina and the Massisipi; was Copyed from a Draught Drawn upon a Deer Skin by an Indian Cacique and Presented to Francis Nicholson Esqr. Governour of Carolina.' Contemporary manuscript copy. *c*. 1723. 114 × 145 cm. Public Record Office, Map Room, Colonial Office 700, North American Colonies, General No. 6 (2). For a facsimile and interpretation, see G. Malcolm Lewis, 'Travelling in Unchartered Territory', in Peter Barber and Christopher Board (eds.), *Tales From the Map Room* (London, 1993), pp. 40–1.

17 Non-Chi-Ning-Ga (Iowa), untitled manuscript map of the Upper Mississippi and Missouri drainage systems between Lake Michigan and the Rocky Mountains showing 'the route of my (Ioway) forefathers – the land that we have always claimed', presented at a council between Indians of the Mississippi and Missouri in Washington, D. C., on 7 Oct. 1837. 104 × 69 cm. National Archives, Cartographic Branch, College Park, Maryland, Record Group 75, Map 821, Tube 520. For a facsimile and interpretation see G. Malcolm Lewis, 'Indian Maps: Their Place in the History of Plains Cartography', in Frederick C. Luebke *et al.* (eds.), *Mapping the North American Plains: Essays in the History of Cartography* (Norman and London, 1987), figs. 4.2 and 4.3, pp. 66–8.

18 Names italicized in the text are in the form in which they appear on the skin map and are used whenever the text refers to it rather than to the ground referents. For the latter non-italicized current spellings are used.

19 Circles, and less frequently semicircles, were often used by Indians to represent native settlements. See, for example, the Chickasaw and Iowa maps cited in nn. 16 and 17.

20 For an easy to assimilate but authoritative series of maps reconstructing settlement patterns in the region see Helen Hornbeck Tanner (ed.), *Atlas of Great Lakes Indian History* (Norman and London, 1987), maps 6, 9, 13, 16, 17, 18, 19, 20 and 21.

21 Wayne C. Temple, 'Indian Villages of the Illinois Country: Historic Tribes', *Illinois State Museum Scientific Papers*, vol. ii, part ii (1958), pp. 34–5.

22 Ibid., p. 66.

23 Ibid., p. 74.

24 Ibid., pp. 81 and 72.

25 Ibid., p. 54.

26 'A treaty between the United States of America and the Kaskaskia Tribe of Indians ... Aug.13, 1803.' Kappler, op. cit., pp. 67–8.

27 In theory, it ought to be possible to make a more precise determination on the basis of the map's settlement symbols. In practice this is virtually impossible for two reasons. First, the topological structure of the drainage network (neither linear scale nor angular direction are conserved) make it impossible to identify the ground sites with sufficient certainty. Secondly, many of the settlements were Indian and some of these were small and/or transitory. Even using the authoritative settlement-pattern reconstructions in Tanner, op. cit., it is not possible to identify most of them. A few, however, are speculatively identified, at later stages in this article.

28 Tanner, op. cit., map 19, p. 93.

29 E.g., the Chickasaw map of *c*. 1723 (n. 16) represents fifteen 'Paths' all of which are essentially straight, even though most were several hundreds of kilometres long and followed courses that were adjusted to the in places difficult terrain.

30 *American State Papers. Documents, Legislative and Executive of the Congress of the United States from the Second Session of the Eleventh to the Third Session of the Thirteenth Congress Inclusive, Class viii: Public Lands*, vol. ii (Washington, 1834), pp. 117–20.

31 Jack M. Sosin, *Whitehall and the Wilderness: the Middle West in British Colonial Policy 1760–1775* (Lincoln, 1961), pp. 229–30.

32 From the records of the East India Company, London, printed in Shaw Livermore, *Early American Land Companies: their Influence on Corporate Development* (New York, 1939), p. 106, n. 69. Pratt, as Lord Camden, was Lord Chancellor from July 1766 to January 1770; Yorke succeeded him briefly in January 1770, but died before being formally created Lord Morden.

33 Sosin, op. cit., p. 231.

34 Copy given by William Murray to Governor Dunmore of Virginia, who forwarded it to the Earl of Dartmouth, Secretary of State for the Colonies, London, Public Record Office, C. O. 5/1352, f. 155; quoted in Sosin, op. cit., p. 231.

35 For an exhaustive review of how colonial land speculators obtained the edited and abbreviated Camden-Yorke Opinion see 'Appendix: The Yorke-Camden Opinion', Sosin, op. cit., pp. 259–67.

36 'Illinois and Wabash Land Companies [a memorial] Communicated to the House of Representatives, on the 21st of December, 1810', and 'Illinois and Wabash Land Companies [a report with recommendation from Jeremiah Morrow, for the Committee on Public Lands] Communicated to the House of Representatives, on the 30th of January, 1811', *American State Papers...*, *Class viii: Public Lands*, vol. ii, pp. 108–17 and 253.

37 For an account of William Murray's activities during the years 1768–73 see Anna E. Marks, 'William Murray, Trader and Land Speculator in the Illinois Country', *Transactions of the Illinois State Historical Society for the Year 1919*, no. xxvi (Springfield, 1920), pp. 188–212, esp. ch. 2: 'William Murray, Trader in Illinois', pp. 191–200.

38 Fort Gage had been established in the previous year at the confluence of the Kaskaskia River with the Missouri. Only a few miles to the south, it was effectively the British successor to the by then abandoned French Fort Chartres, to which Murray had first gone as a trader in 1768. Although the British military regime was new, Murray would have had many key civilian and Indian contacts in the several white settlements and Indian villages hereabouts (including the Spanish settlements of Ste Genevieve and New Bourbon on the west bank of the Mississippi) and in the vast territory to the east extending across what is now southern and central Illinois to the Wabash valley beyond.

39 Marks, 'William Murray', p. 200.

40 Ibid., p. 201.

41 Quoted in Marks, 'William Murray', p. 202.

42 Published retrospectively in several places, the 1773 and 1775 deeds of purchase are printed consecutively in *American State Papers... Class viii: Public Lands*, vol. ii, pp. 117–20. But see also n. 45.

43 Ste Genevieve, on the west bank of the Mississippi River only a little above Kaskaskia, had been established in 1739, thirty-six years after the latter.

44 Marks, 'William Murray', p. 204.

45 Printed versions of both the deeds vary somewhat. That used in the following analysis of the Wabash purchase is reproduced in *American State Papers... Class ii: Indian Affairs*, vol. iv (Washington, 1832), pp. 338–40.

46 The precise number of Indians is unclear. The deed begins by naming eleven (1 *supra*). The signatories, however, include only eight of these, plus two others not mentioned at the beginning.

47 *American State Papers... Class ii: Indian Affairs*, vol. iv, pp. 339–40.

48 René Jetté, *Dictionnaire généalogique des familles du Québec des origines à 1730* (Montreal, 1983), p. 125. Fort St Joseph was located in what is now southwest Michigan close to what was then the main Miami village.

49 Marthe Fairbault-Beauregard, *La Population des forts français d'Amérique, XVIIIe siècle...* (Montreal, 1982), vol. i, p. 180.

50 I am indebted to Richard Day of the Lewis Historical Library, Vincennes University, for this and other information relating to the Bolons; letter to the author franked 25 Aug. 1994. The memorial is included in the Gage Manuscripts, William L. Clements Library, Ann Arbor.

51 In 1806 'H. Bolon' was listed as an 'employee of the Indian Department'. With a salary of $365.00 per annum he was 'Interpreter' for the 'Peorias, "Loups", "Shavans", [and] Kickapoos'; letter from Pierre Chouteau to Gen. Atkinson, St Louis, 12 Apr. 1806. The French original is in St Louis, Missouri Historical Society, Pierre Chouteau Letterbook, pp. 87–93.

An English translation is printed in Abraham P. Nasatir (ed.), *Before Lewis and Clark: Documents Illustrating the History of the Missouri 1785–1804* (St Louis, 1952), vol. ii, pp. 767–71. See also n. 55.

52 The 'B' is certain, and the 'H' is almost certain. See also n. 1.

53 For a discussion of the linguistic relationships between these three tribes see Ives Goddard, 'Central Algonquian Languages', and for the political relationships between them see Charles Callendar, 'Miami', in Bruce G. Trigger (ed.), *Northeast*, William C. Sturtevant (gen. ed.), *Handbook of North American Indians*, vol. xv (Washington, 1978), pp. 585 and 682.

54 Ibid., p. 686.

55 These and other details are contained in the letter of 25 Apr. 1994 from Richard Day of Vincennes University, for which see n. 50. There is, however, some doubt about Hypolite Bolon's later life. Hence the 'apparently' in the main text. According to one source, he was buried at Ste Geneviève on 25 March 1795: Katherine W. Seineke, *The George Rogers Clark Adventure in the Illinois and Selected Documents of the American Revolution at the Frontier Posts* (New Orleans, 1981), p. 600. If this was so, then the Hypolite Bolon, Indian interpreter, whose name was associated with St Louis at the end of the eighteenth century and until as late as 1806 could well have been the son legitimated in Vincennes on 28 September 1786 when he was approximately six years old and whose mother was apparently the Delaware woman whom Hypolite Bolon senior had married on the same day after the dispensation of banns. By 1806, however, Hypolite Bolon junior would have been only about twenty-six years old and unlikely to have merited the $365.00 annual salary paid to him by the Indian Department, concerning which see n. 51.

56 Kappler, *Indian Treaties*, p. 77.

57 The name 'Wia' ( = Wea), positioned to the east of the upper-middle course of the Wabash, might be taken to indicate that the Piankashaw had no right to sell land there, even though in the deed, to which there were apparently no Wea signatories, they undoubtedly did. This must have been negotiated at a later stage or with a different subgroup.

58 The dotted straight line parallel to the Wabash River and approximately but not precisely separating its basin from that of the Mississippi-Kaskaskia-Illinois may have been drawn to indicate schematically the eastern boundary of the Illinois Land Company's purchase. Its role would probably have been to confirm to the Piankashaw Indians that a purchase had been made but that even when settled by whites there would still be a large intervening area of unsold land available for hunting.

59 In the absence of printing on the frontier and two hundred years before photocopying and faxing, discussions involving representatives of subgroups and conducted over a period of time as part of a larger network of negotiations would require multiple hand-executed working documents, of which there could well have been variants. Those produced for literate parties might be expected to include written content.

60 'Piankishwa Sold' positioned thereabouts suggests finality and the purchase deed did indeed embrace this area. Conversely, although the deed included a large area to the east of the lower Wabash River, the skin map is silent about it. This could be interpreted as having resulted from its purchase having been negotiated later and/or having involved a different subgroup of interested parties.

61 Three observations are pertinent here. First, only a very small area of land immediately opposite Post Vincennes is shown outside the dotted lines inferred to be the boundaries of land being negotiated for sale. It gives the impression of being a mere corridor intended perhaps to guarantee access to and from Kaskaskia via the road (straight line) linking it to Post Vincennes via prairies that at that date were not in the process of being purchased. Secondly, in the deed of purchase the 'mere corridor' to the west of Post Vincennes had become a twenty-four-league-wide gap 'reserved for [use by] the inhabitants of Post Vincennes'. What had first been intended as a corridor for the use of all would appear to have become half of a much larger preserve for French residents, the other part of which was to the east of the Wabash River. Finally, on the skin map the belt to the north of the 'corridor' is slightly wider than that to the south, whereas, according to the terms of the deed of purchase, the belt to the north of the 'gap' is defined as thirty leagues wide; slightly narrower than the thirty-five-league-wide belt to the south of it. In the course of subsequent

86

negotiations, the relative widths of the north-western and southwestern belts would appear to have been reversed.

62 In addition to neat small holes and larger torn holes at various places near the periphery of the skin, of which there are no equivalents elsewhere, there are four even larger rust-stained holes, one at each corner of the skin. The latter could be older than the others and probably indicates that the map was nailed to a vertical surface, perhaps for a time in wet conditions, for use in some kind of council.

63 This and subsequent information about John Mullanphy is from Hyde and Conard (eds.), op. cit., pp. 1591–3.

64 John Mullanphy had a 'thorough knowledge of French', ibid., p. 1592.

65 English translation of letter from Cerré to George Clark, St Genevieve, 11 July 1778. Printed in Clarence W. Alvord (ed.), 'Kaskaskia Records 1778–1790', *Collections of the Illinois State Historical Library*, vol. v, *Virginia Series*, vol. ii (Springfield, Illinois, 1909), p. 49.

66 The seven 'inquiries' and Cerré's 'answers' are reproduced in Walter B. Douglas, 'Jean Gabriel Cerré – a Sketch', *Transactions of the Illinois State Historical Society for the Year 1903* (Springfield, Illinois, 1904), pp. 286–8.

67 Ibid., p. 283.

68 Ibid.

69 See n. 55 for a preliminary discussion of whether the 'H. Bolon' associated with the St Louis region as late as 1806 was Hypolite Bolon senior or his son with the same name. Although that H. Bolon was stated to be an interpreter to the 'Peorias, "Loups", "Shavans", and Kickapoos', rather than to the Piankashaws, all but the Loups spoke central Algonquian languages similar to Piankashaw. The Loups of the Ohio valley were mainly Delawares, of which people Hypolite Bolon senior's wife was a member. Hence, he was almost certainly a speaker of Unami and/or some other closely related eastern Algonquian language. It seems very likely, therefore, that it was indeed Hypolite Bolon senior who on 13 Nov. 1799 entered into an agreement to purchase a lot in St Louis and have a small house built on it: Charles E. Peterson, 'The Houses of French St Louis', *Missouri Historical Society Bulletin* (Apr. 1947), p. 144. At the time of that agreement he would appear to have been a resident of Aux Salines, near Ste Genevieve on the Mississippi some sixty miles south of St Louis. From that place in 1799 he donated twelve 'piastres' to aid Spain in the final stage of the defence from French interests of its territory west of the Missouri River: Louis Houck (ed.), *The Spanish Regime in Missouri*, vol. ii (Chicago, 1909), p. 293.

70 Kappler, op. cit., pp. 74–6.

71 Nasatir, vol. ii, p. 771.

72 Hyde and Conard, op. cit., pp. 1591–2.

73 Ibid., op. cit., p. 1592.

74 George P. Winship (ed.), 'Translation of the Letter from Coronado to Mendoza, August 3, 1540', in 'The Coronado Expedition, 1540–1542', *Fourteenth Annual Report of the Bureau of Ethnology to the Secretary of the Smithsonian Institution 1892–1893*, pt. i (Washington, 1896), pp. 558 and 592.

75 Reuben G. Thwaites (ed.), *Original Journals of the Lewis and Clark Expedition* (Cleveland, 1904), vol. vii, pp. 202–4.

76 Quinepeno, a Mississauga chief, speaking at a meeting on the Credit River, west of Toronto, between representatives of his people and William Claus, Deputy Superintendent of Upper Canada. Ottawa, National Archives of Canada, MS. Indian Affairs, Lieutenant-Governor's Office - Upper Canada, Correspondence 1796–1806, Record Group 10, vol. i, p. 298.

77 John C. Fitzpatrick (ed.), *The Diaries of George Washington 1748–1799* (Boston, 1925), vol. i, p. 439.

78 Tanner, op. cit., especially maps 16 and 19.

# BENJAMIN FRANKLIN AND THE SNAKE THAT WOULD NOT DIE

KAREN SEVERUD COOK

ON 9 May 1754 an article was published in Benjamin Franklin's newspaper, *The Pennsylvania Gazette*, calling for the British colonies on North America's eastern seaboard to unite against the threat of French aggression from the western interior. This rousing exhortation was echoed by an accompanying illustration depicting the British colonies as a snake cut into segments and was captioned, 'JOIN, or DIE' (fig. 1). Although often cited as the first political cartoon published in an American newspaper, this illustration has rarely received more than passing mention. The frequent inaccuracies in such citations inspired (or rather irritated) Albert Matthews to write the only detailed historical study of the original snake cartoon and its subsequent variants.[1] Even Matthews, however, failed to make the important observation that the snake cartoon is a map.

Admittedly, it is so unconventional that even historians of cartography have failed to see it as a map, although it has a number of cartographic features. The eight segments of the snake are labelled with the initials of the colonies in geographical order, from 'N.E.' for New England at its head to 'S.C.' for South Carolina at its tail. Thus, the snake map retains the topological quality of neighbourship; places next to one another on the ground are next to one another on the map. Further, the undulations of the snake suggest the curving shape of the eastern seacoast of North America, even if one could not superimpose the cartoon on a map and match the shapes precisely. The diagonal position of the snake suggests the southwest to northeast direction of that coastline. The image is also maplike in being a vertical plan rather than an oblique view. Even though it lacks the planimetric accuracy expected of conventional maps, it is a map. Or rather, it is a cartographic caricature, a distorted representation exaggerating the subject's most striking features. Before assessing its significance as a map, though, it is necessary to know more about the cartoon and its history.

The purpose of this article is to trace the antecedents and influence of Franklin's cartoon. Its progeny were numerous, because the cartoon was immediately copied in other colonial newspapers. The snake cartoon was also repeatedly revived and its message adapted to new political circumstances: the Stamp Act crisis in the 1760s, the American Revolution in the 1770s and, finally, the American Civil War in the 1860s.

88

*Fig. 1.* The original snake cartoon from *The Pennsylvania Gazette*, 9 May 1754. From A. Matthews, *The Snake Devices*, 1908. BL, 011902.f.84

### AUTHORSHIP AND ANTECEDENTS

Although the news article and the cartoon are unsigned, Benjamin Franklin almost certainly was their creator. His position as co-owner of *The Pennsylvania Gazette* provided the editorial opportunity and his known concern for colonial union the incentive to contribute the article. By 1754 Franklin, aged forty-eight, had reduced his active participation in business and had more time to pursue his interests in science and politics.[2] On 8 April 1754 the Governor of Pennsylvania had appointed Franklin a commissioner to the congress of colonial delegates meeting on 19 June at Albany to settle a defence treaty with the Indian tribes of the Six Nations. During the journey to Albany Franklin drafted a proposal for the union of the colonies which the Albany Congress later approved, although the plan was never implemented.[3] The 9 May article in *The Pennsylvania Gazette* with its motto, 'JOIN, or DIE', and its warning about the French threat, indicates that Franklin already had the benefits of union in mind:

… many more French are expected from Canada; the Design being to establish themselves, settle their Indians, and build Forts just on the Back of our Settlements in all our Colonies; from which Forts, as they did from Crown-Point, they may send out their Parties to kill and scalp the Inhabitants, and ruin the Frontier Colonies. … The confidence of the French in this Undertaking seems well-grounded on the present disunited State of the British Colonies, and the extreme Difficulty of bringing so many different Governments and Assemblies to agree in any speedy and effectual Measures for our common Defence and Security; while our Enemies have the very great Advantage of being under one Direction, with one Council, and one Purse. Hence, and from the great Distance of Britain, they presume that they may with Impunity violate the most solemn Treaties subsisting between the two Crowns, kill, seize and imprison our Traders, and confiscate their Effects at Pleasure (as they have done for several Years past), murder and scalp our Farmers,

*Non Votis, &c.*

*Fig. 2.* The frontispiece to Benjamin Franklin's pamphlet, *Plain Truth*, 1747. BL, 103.k.62

with their Wives and Children, and take an easy Possession of such Parts of the British Territory as they find most convenient for them; which if they are permitted to do, must end in the Destruction of the British Interest, Trade and Plantations in America.[4]

Franklin had made innovative use of a cartoon once before to accent his political writings. In 1747 he had printed and distributed a pamphlet urging Pennsylvanians to prepare for their own defence, as he later recalled:

With respect to Defence, Spain having been several Years at War against Britain, and being at length join'd by France, which brought us into greater Danger; and the laboured & long-continued Endeavours of our Governor Thomas to prevail with our Quaker Assembly to pass a Militia Law, & make other Provisions for the Security of the Province having proved abortive, I determined to try what might be done by a voluntary Association of the People. To promote this I first wrote & published a Pamphlet, intitled, PLAIN TRUTH, in which I stated our defenceless situation in strong Lights, with the Necessity of Union & Discipline for our Defence, and promis'd to propose in a few Days an Association to be generally signed for that purpose. The Pamphlet had a sudden & surprizing Effect. ... the Subscribers amounted at length to upwards of Ten Thousand.[5]

The frontispiece of *Plain Truth* (fig. 2) shows a kneeling wagon-driver praying to the god Hercules, while his team of three horses struggles to pull a heavily laden wagon out of the mud. An explanation is provided by the accompanying Latin text, 'Non votis, neque suppliciis muliebribus, auxilia deorum parantur', translated in the second edition of *Plain Truth* as, 'Divine assistance and protection are not to be obtained by timorous prayers, and womanish supplications'.[6] The illustration comes from a set of twelve cuts purchased by Franklin to enliven the fables in his printing of Thomas Dilworth's school book, *A New Guide to the English Tongue*, in Philadelphia in 1747.[7] Inventively used again in *Plain Truth*, the cut of the foolish wagon driver became the first political cartoon of any kind to be published in America.

The success of the *Plain Truth* cartoon may have inspired Franklin to use a second cartoon, the snake map, in 1754 to arouse support for colonial union. Franklin sent the snake cartoon to Richard Partridge, the Pennsylvania agent in London, on 8 May 1754 (the day before its publication in *The Pennsylvania Gazette*) saying, 'With this I send you a Paragraph of News from our Gazette, with an Emblem printed therewith, which it may be well to get inserted in some of your most publick Papers.'[8] Although no instance is known of the use of the cartoon in an English paper, it was copied in four Boston and New York papers within weeks of its appearance in Pennsylvania.

Franklin invented a third political cartoon, 'MAGNA Britannia: her Colonies REDUC'D', in London during the winter of 1765–6 and circulated it to gain support for the repeal of the Stamp Act.[9] His appreciation of the cartoon as an effective medium of communication must have been in his mind in 1773 when he observed that 'Odd ways of presenting Matters to the publick View sometimes occasion them to be more read, talk'd of, and more attended to.'[10]

He also created symbolic designs for various other purposes. His account of the response to *Plain Truth* in 1747 continues with the information that, 'The Women, by Subscriptions among themselves, provided Silk Colours, which they presented to the [militia] Companies, painted with different Devices and Mottoes which I supplied.'[11] The tradition that Franklin contributed to the design of American paper currency in 1775–6 is supported by the discovery, among his papers, of drawings in his hand of the emblem used on the back of the bills: a circle of thirteen links, each representing a colony and labelled in geographical sequence.[12]

Whether Franklin actually engraved the snake cartoon is more problematical, although it is certain that he did some relief and intaglio engraving during his early career. He may have acquired this skill while apprenticed to his elder brother, James, a London-trained Boston printer also identified as the probable engraver of some woodcuts.[13] Recollecting the various tasks he had performed while foreman for the Philadelphia printer, Samuel Keimer, after returning from England in 1726, Franklin wrote, 'I also engrav'd several Things on occasion.'[14] Employed again by Keimer in 1728 to print paper currency in New Jersey, Franklin remembered that 'I contrived a Copper-Plate Press for it, the first that had been seen in the Country. I cut several Ornaments and Checks for the Bills.'[15] A receipt in Franklin's accounts indicates that he may have cut the wood block for a map in 1733.[16] However, as Franklin's own printing business grew in the 1740s, he began to purchase small cuts and ornaments rather than make them himself.[17] It is possible that he commissioned James Turner, a Boston engraver of maps and other illustrations known to have worked for him, to cut the snake cartoon.[18] Lacking conclusive evidence, we have to leave this question open.

As the author of the snake cartoon, if not its engraver, Franklin drew upon various sources for its form and content. The snake cartoon follows the formula of the standard emblem book, a type of literature that had originated during the sixteenth century in Italy and soon thereafter spread across Europe. Conventionally in the emblem book each example consisted of three parts: motto, symbolic picture and explanatory text. Readers enjoyed deciphering the symbolic meaning and relationship of the elements. For example, in the 1564 Lyons edition of Andreas Alciatus's *Emblemata*, one of many editions of this popular work, the motto, 'Ex literarum Studiis immortalitate acquiri (From literary studies comes immortality)', is illustrated by a Triton encircled by a snake (representing eternity) and is explained by lines of poetry and prose below.[19] By the eighteenth century, however, the emblem book had degenerated from a serious literary genre into a cheap formula used chiefly for education in children's books and entertainment in humorous reading matter for adults.[20]

In this latter guise the emblem was also employed by the political satirists who flourished in eighteenth-century England, but whose origins can be traced several centuries earlier. Where the emblem in its pure form had been an end in itself, political satire delivered its message with a purpose. Pictorial propaganda mocking authority, such as by showing the Pope as the Devil, had been used effectively by Martin Luther during the Reformation. Later Holland became a source of satirical prints whose anti-Spanish, anti-Jesuit viewpoint was well-received in England. While Dutch prints continued to circulate, English-produced prints began to appear in the seventeenth century, chiefly as an expression of opposition to the government.[21]

Benjamin Franklin had had ample opportunity to become familiar with the various types of emblem literature. The first book he bought as a child in Boston, according to his autobiography, was John Bunyan's *The Pilgrim's Progress*, a late example, even at its first publication in 1678, of serious literature employing emblematic symbolism.[22] Throughout his childhood, apprenticeship and early working years in Boston (1706–23), Philadelphia (1723–4) and London (1724–6), Franklin had supplemented his early formal schooling with voracious and wide-ranging reading, drawing on the libraries of acquaintances and paying to borrow books from booksellers.[23] A developing interest in linguistic symbolism was indicated by the sixteen-year-old Franklin's fascination with John Wilkins's *An Essay towards a Real Character and a Philosophical Language* (London, 1668), a book proposing a philosophical subject classification represented by a shorthand symbolic language.[24] Thus it seems hardly surprising that in 1751 Franklin was the first to publish an American edition of Johann Arndt's *Sechs gestreiche Bücher von Wahren Christenthum*, a German book of symbolic devices popular among German settlers in Pennsylvania.[25] Typical of colonial printing establishments, the business built up by Franklin in Philadelphia during the 1730s and 1740s included the importing and selling of books, maps and related items, as well as jobbing printing and newspaper and book publishing. He was the leading founder of the Library Company of Philadelphia in 1731 and was instrumental during the following decades in the selection and acquisition of books for what was, in effect, the city's first public library.[26] As his circumstances improved, Franklin was able to become a collector of books himself. He amassed a substantial personal library in Philadelphia even before the extensive acquisitions made during his later lengthy stays in England (1757–75) and France (1776–85). The catalogue of his personal library has disappeared since his death, and only about a quarter of the library's contents have since been traced.[27] However, it is reasonable to assume that by 1754 (the year of the snake cartoon) he already had a wide knowledge of both American and foreign publications.

Not only does Franklin's snake cartoon employ the emblematic formula of motto, symbolic picture and emblematic text, but he also referred to it as an 'Emblem' when he sent it to the Pennsylvania agent in London.[28] Franklin's consciousness of its emblematic character is also supported by his grandson's reference to his later political cartoon, 'MAGNA Britannia: her Colonies REDUC'D', as an 'emblematic design'. William Temple Franklin added that the emblem was printed both by itself on cards and 'on half sheets of paper, with the *explanation* and *moral*'.[29] The text of the explanation, which survives in a later copy, calls the picture a 'Prophetical Emblem'.[30] Joseph Galloway, who received Franklin's political card in 1766, wrote, 'The lance from the thigh of New England, pointed at the breast of Britannia, is striking, as is indeed every other emblem'.[31] In addition to using the word 'emblem', Galloway's comment demonstrates the impact of the pictorial symbolism.

The pictorial imagery in the snake cartoon incorporates several symbolic themes whose combined interpretation amplifies and reinforces the text: map, snake and dismemberment themes. In an investigation of Franklin's sources, each theme warrants separate consideration.

*The Map Theme*

All available evidence indicates that Franklin was very aware of the value of maps as a means of recording and communicating geographical information. He bought and sold maps as part of his printing business,[32] exchanged maps with friends,[33] participated in smuggling maps out of England during the American Revolution,[34] used maps himself, supported the production of new maps and even participated in mapmaking. For instance, it was Franklin who was asked by the Pennsylvania Assembly in 1747 to order large maps, some with bordering views, for display in 'the long Gallery and the Assembly Room in the Statehouse'.[35] Franklin was also a friend and financial backer of the cartographer, Lewis Evans.[36] And when in 1753 Franklin, who since 1737 had been Deputy Postmaster of Philadelphia, was appointed Deputy Postmaster General of the American colonies, he improved the efficiency of the post routes forming the main intercolonial communication network, a task which required the knowledge and use of maps.[37] Still holding that post in 1768 while based in London, where he had been the Pennsylvania agent since 1757, Franklin was consulted about the reasons for British mail packets from London taking two weeks longer to sail to New York than to Rhode Island, a delay not explicable simply by relative distance. Ships sailing to New York were being slowed by the Gulf Stream, a phenomenon of the ocean current already familiar to American seamen. Franklin then asked his cousin, Timothy Folger, a Nantucket sea captain, to mark the 'Dimentions Course and Swiftness of the Stream' on a chart and had it printed for use by packet captains. This chart was an important early example of thematic cartography.[38]

Franklin's article in *The Pennsylvania Gazette* on 9 May 1754 vividly conjures up his mental map of the British colonies as a narrow strip 'confined to the country between the sea and the mountains', threatened at their rear by French expansion into 'the great country back of the Appalachian mountains'.[39] His familiarity with military maps and tactics comes across as he visualizes the coastal colonies as a defensive line vulnerable to attack from the rear.

Franklin's knowledge of maps of the British colonies may well have been matched by exposure to symbolic maps used in political satire. One early example printed in 1566 in Geneva and dedicated to England's Queen Elizabeth was the anti-Catholic '*Mappemonde nouvelle papistique*', a sixteen-sheet print showing a world map symbolically poised in the jaws of Hell. At least two other satirical maps relating to political events in England were produced in Amsterdam during the seventeeth century.[40] Further there were cartographic personifications of European countries. In some cases the map, signifying the territory ruled, adorned a person. The female personification of 'Great Britaine' shown in the titlepiece of Drayton's *Poly-Olbion* in 1613 is wearing a map.[41] Similarly, one of the few surviving English prints about the seventeenth-century conflict with France shows Louis XIV attired in 'the Usurper's Habit', a costume covered with depictions of battles, towns and fortresses and holding his hat, which represents Limerick.[42] In other instances, the person or animal was embodied in the map. For example, the numerous cartographic portrayals of Europe as a queen and of *Leo Belgicus* are well known.

### The Snake Theme

The use of a person, animal or object to represent a concept was a typical emblematic device,[43] although the historical roots of the practice certainly lay deeper, for animal personifications are universally typical of folk tales.[44] Snakes have always been central figures in myth and fable, sometimes associated with good and sometimes with evil.[45] Such symbolism, the cumulated heritage of preceding ages and cultures, was consciously revived by the Renaissance and later creators of emblem designs.

The heraldic association of different animals with particular countries was already widespread when the political cartoons of the seventeenth and eighteenth centuries gave this form of personification a satirical twist. By the 1660s England was being depicted as a lion or a dog in Dutch political prints, while the Commonwealth under Oliver Cromwell appeared as a dragon. Political cartoons during the French and Indian War often pitted the British lion against the Gallic cock.[46] The possibilities for animal representation had been expanded by the opening up of the New World. The rattlesnake, indigenous to America, had become a symbolic attribute of the New World, along with other animals, like the alligator and the armadillo, in pictorial representations of the Continents.

Typical of early scientific writing, the first accounts of American animals tended to blend folklore and fact. The myth, carried from Europe, that snakes cut into pieces could rejoin or regenerate missing parts was based on a confusion between snakes and certain lizards which, as a defence mechanism, can lose their tails and regrow them.[47] This myth was probably the source for the image of a snake divided into two parts which appears in Nicolas Verrien's *Livre curieux et utile* (fig. 3), an emblem book first published about 1685 in Paris.[48] The accompanying motto, 'se rejoindre ou mourir', must have been the source for Franklin's 'Join, or die'. However, the snake emblem of Verrien is much smaller and more generalized than Franklin's snake cartoon, and Franklin must have had other, more detailed snake images in mind, as well. Mark Catesby, whose *The Natural History of Carolina, Florida and the Bahama Islands* published in London 1731–43 stands out as a landmark in the natural-history literature of North America, describes the habits of rattlesnakes:

They are the most inactive and slow moving Snake of all others, and are never Aggressors, except in what they prey upon, for unless they are disturbed they will not bite, and when provoked, they give Warning by shaking their Rattle. These are commonly believed to be the most deadly venomous Serpent of any in these parts of America ...[49]

Benjamin Franklin may have had Catesby's description in mind when he contributed a satirical piece to *The Pennsylvania Gazette* on 9 May 1751. In it he suggested that in return for the 'Thieves and Villains introduc'd among us' by the British 'Exporting of Felons to the Colonies', the colonies might send to England 'Numbers of these venomous Reptiles we call RATTLE-SNAKES; Felons-convict from the Beginning of the World', concluding:

That this Exporting of Felons to the colonies may be consider'd as a Trade, as well in the Light of a Favour. Now all Commerce implies *Returns*: Justice requires them: There can be no Trade without them. And Rattle-Snakes seem the most *suitable returns* for the *Human Serpents* sent us by our *Mother* Country. In this, however, as in every other Branch of Trade, she will have the Advantage of us. She will reap *equal* Benefits without equal Risque of the Inconveniencies and Dangers. For the *Rattle-Snake* gives Warning before he attempts his Mischief; which the Convict does not.[50]

It seems likely that snake illustrations in Catesby's books were the direct pictorial source, as well, for Franklin's snake cartoon in 1754. This connection is not immediately apparent from the first and best-known plate, 'The Rattle-Snake', shown coiled in the classic 'don't-tread-on-me' pose of symbolic (but non-cartographic) rattlesnake representations. However, the next plate of 'The Small Rattle-Snake' (Plate VIII),

95

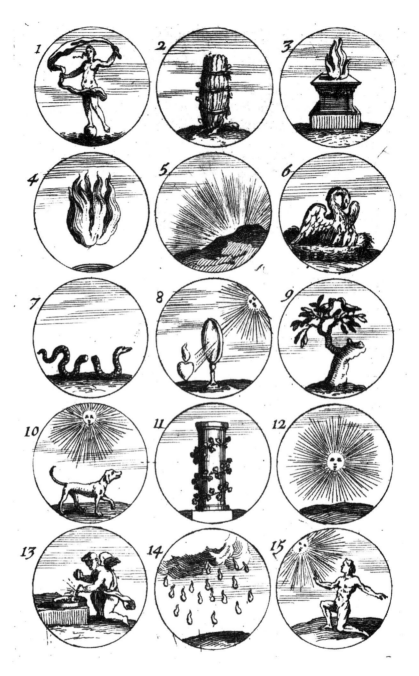

*Fig. 3.* Emblems from Nicolas Verrien's *Livre curieux et utile*, including no. 7, the divided snake, with the motto 'Se rejoindre ou mourir'

96

open-mouthed with projecting forked tongue in an undulating pose, is very similar to the Franklin cartoon. On the other hand, the snake in the Franklin cartoon may not be a rattlesnake; the indeterminate markings near the tip of its tail could simply be scales. Other distinctive features of the cartoon snake, however, appear elsewhere in Catesby's book. The single loop of the cartoon snake's body matches that of 'The Green Spotted Snake'. The plate of 'The Chain Snake' shows a dark blue snake apparently divided into segments by thin yellow bands, an effect strikingly similar to the cut segments in the snake cartoon. Finally, the description of 'The Glass Snake' says, 'A small Blow with a Stick will cause the Body to separate, not only at the Place struck, but at two or three other Places; the Muscles being articulated in a singular Manner quite through to the Vertebra.'[51] One can imagine Franklin drawing an analogy with the idea that a blow to one of the colonies would hurt them all. Rather than copying a single snake illustration, it seems that Franklin used a composite of features from a number of snake images and descriptions.

### The Dismemberment Theme

The idea of a personification cut into segments may have had other sources, as well. The depiction of an animal or human personification of a country being dismembered or trampled was also common imagery in the political print. Henry Stubbe wrote angrily in 1672 that Dutch satirical prints and medals showing a prostrate Britannia trampled by the elephant of Holland or depicting ruffians cutting the tails off English dogs were ample provocation for war.[52] During the mid-eighteenth century British political cartoons regularly showed Britannia being murdered or butchered. It is likely, for example, that Franklin knew 'The Conduct, of the two B[utche]rs', a pictorial attack on the Pelham brothers (First Lord of the Treasury and Secretary of State respectively) published in 1749. That print shows Britannia being dismembered and disembowelled, and her severed arms bear the geographical names of Cape Breton and Gibraltar. Along with a 1756 cartoon showing 'The English Lion Dismember'd', it is thought to have been the design source for Franklin's third political cartoon, 'MAGNA Britannia: her Colonies REDUC'D', issued in 1766.[53]

As with map imagery, Franklin used similar dissection imagery in his writings. When General Edward Braddock brought British troops to America in 1755 and was preparing to advance inland to subdue the French and Indians, Franklin sent him the following advice:

The only Danger I apprehend of Obstruction to your March, is from the Ambuscades of Indians, who by constant Practice are dextrous in laying and executing them. And the slender Line near four Miles long, which your Army must make, may expose it to be attack'd by Surprize in its Flanks, and to be cut like a Thread into several Pieces, which from their Distance cannot come up in time to support each other.[54]

In July 1755 Braddock's troops were ambushed after crossing the Monongahela River, much as Franklin had predicted.

Unlike the frontispiece in *Plain Truth*, the snake cartoon seems to have been an original design, drawing upon the various sources just described. Its publication in a newspaper in 1754 was equally remarkable. Several factors discouraged the use of pictures in eighteenth-century American newspapers: the scarcity and high cost both of engravers capable of cutting pictorial printing blocks and of paper on which to print them. Illustrations were usually limited to the masthead design or to small stock images, such as horses, houses or ships, identifying types of advertisements.[55] Only exceptional circumstances, combined with Franklin's awareness of the power of the graphic image to enhance the printed word, could have given birth to the snake cartoon.

It is likely that Franklin published the snake cartoon just five weeks before the Albany Congress as part of a deliberate strategy to gain support for his proposal for colonial union. After all, he had successfully employed similar tactics with his political pamphlet *Plain Truth* in 1747. As a newspaper publisher, Franklin was ideally placed to reach a wide audience. Newspaper publishing had been introduced to the American colonies earlier in the eighteenth century and was catering to an increasingly literate general public. Typically located in a coastal town, the colonial newspaper publisher used commercial contacts to import news from Europe along with trade goods. As well as printing local items and advertisements, the colonial newspaper redistributed news from overseas and from other colonies. The colonial newspaper became a forum for public discourse and contributed to the formation of an American political consciousness. Prior to the American Revolution, newspaper articles written by a relatively small number of political activists made publicly voiced discontent seem general.[56] Set in that context, it is not surprising that Franklin regarded his political writings as a means to an end. He expressed his pragmatic attitude in a letter to his sister, Jane Mecom, in 1767:

You desire me to send you all the political Pieces I have been the Author of. I have never kept them. They were most of them written occasionally for transient Purposes, and having done their Business, they die and are forgotten. I could as easily make a Collection for you of all the past Parings of my Nails.[57]

Ephemeral or not, Franklin's snake cartoon had considerable public exposure. Re-engraved versions appeared with variants of the text in *The New-York Gazette* and *The New-York Mercury* on 13 May 1754, in *The Boston Gazette* on 21 May and in *The Boston News-Letter* on 23 May. The design of the cartoon as copied varies only slightly from the original; the added slogan, 'Unite and Conquer', issues from the mouth of the snake in the Boston versions. Only a couple of papers published the text without the snake cartoon, *The Pennsylvania Journal* on 9 May and *The Boston Evening-Post* on 20 May. On 19 July *The Virginia Gazette* mentioned the snake cartoon but did not reproduce it. *The South Carolina Gazette* of 22 August printed an article with a much-simplified diagram of the snake cartoon, formed by short lengths of printer's rule labelled with the initials of the colonies in the same geographical sequence.[58]

Despite whatever support this rapid and wide newspaper circulation raised, Franklin's political aim of colonial union was not fulfilled in 1754. Although the representatives of seven colonies who met at Albany that June and July accepted Franklin's plan in principle, the colonial assemblies and the British government were never able to agree on its implementation. Franklin recollected, 'The *Assemblies* did not adopt it as they all thought there was too much Prerogative in it; and in England it was judg'd to have too much of the *Democratic*.'[59] However, the snake map had captured the popular imagination, as its revival in coming decades was to show. As the political situation evolved, both the form of the snake cartoon and the content of its patriotic message changed correspondingly.

### THE STAMP ACT CRISIS

In the 1750s Franklin had sought to unite Britain's American colonies against the French and Indian threat. But when in 1763 the British government began to consider imposing a stamp tax on the American colonies to raise revenue for their defence, the colonial press reacted strongly against it. The newspaper publishers' own interests were threatened, since the proposed tax was to be levied on paper, as well as on other imported goods. With their close ties to England, colonial printers had heard about or experienced personally the harsh taxes imposed on paper in England by the Stamp Acts of 1712 and 1725.[60] The British government now became the oppressor against whom colonial public opinion was to be rallied, and newspaper accounts emphasized the threat posed by taxation to the liberty and livelihood of the colonists in general.[61]

During the unsettled period preceding the imposition of the Stamp Act on 1 November 1765, there appeared on 21 September in New York an opposition publication in the guise of a newspaper, *The Constitutional Courant*. The masthead of *The Constitutional Courant* includes the snake cartoon with the single motto 'JOIN or DIE' as its central feature. The imprint of the paper reads: 'Printed by ANDREW MARVEL, at the Sign of the Bribe refused, on Constitution Hill, North-America.' Andrew Marvel was the pseudonym of William Goddard, a printer who had recently left Providence, Rhode Island, for New York City, associating briefly with several printers there before moving to Philadelphia in December 1766. He is thought to have printed *The Constitutional Courant* at the press of James Parker, located in Woodbridge, New Jersey, in September 1765. Copies were transported secretly to New York City for sale by hawkers and created such a commotion that an official enquiry was held. *The Constitutional Courant* was quickly reprinted in Boston and possibly in New York or Philadelphia in at least two variant editions illustrated with different cuts of the snake cartoon. The Boston version was probably printed by Thomas and John Flett, the publishers of *The Boston Evening-Post*; on 7 October 1765 their paper carried an advertisement for *The Constitutional Courant* using the same cut of the snake cartoon.[62]

The publication on 21 September 1765 of *The Constitutional Courant* may have been timed to influence popular opinion just before the meeting in October of twenty-seven

99

colonial representatives at the Stamp Act Congress held at New York City.[63] If so, it followed the pattern set by Benjamin Franklin with *Plain Truth* in 1747 and the snake cartoon in 1754. As for its content, *The Constitutional Courant* generally voiced, albeit in less temperate language, the conclusions that the Stamp Act Congress would reach. The Congress issued a statement of the rights and liberties of the British American Colonists, pledging allegiance to King George III but calling for the reversal of recent Acts of Parliament, including the Stamp Act, which threatened their rights, liberty and prosperity.[64] *The Constitutional Courant* had similarly implied that the colonies ought to unite in opposition to the British government but stopped short of advocating their political union.

Benjamin Franklin was engaged in anti-Stamp Act lobbying in London and only a distant spectator when *The Constitutional Courant* appeared in 1765. An old and more conservative-minded friend, Cadwallader Colden, sent him a copy of *The Constitutional Courant* from New York on 1 October 1765. Writing in his capacity as Lieutenant Governor of the colony of New York, Colden told Franklin, a Deputy Postmaster General since 1753, of the illicit use of the postal service to deliver the paper:

My regard to you makes me give you the trouble of the inclosed Printed Paper, one or more bundles of which I am well informed were delivered to the Post Rider at Woodbridge by James Parker were distributed by the Post Riders in several parts of this Colony & I believe likewise in the neighbouring Colonies: the doing of which was kept secret from the Post Master in this Place. It is believed that this Paper was printed by Parker after the Printers in this Place had refused to do it, perhaps you may be able to judge from the Types. As he is Secretary to the General Post office in America, I am under a necessity of takeing notice of it to the Secretary of State by the return of the Packet which is daily expected, & I am unwilling to do this without giving you previous notice by a Merchant Ship which Sails Tomorrow.[65]

Colden's sympathies with the British government became even clearer later in October 1765 when he tried to force acceptance of a shipment of stamped paper from England and was consequently burned in effigy by a New York mob.[66]

Once the Stamp Act had been passed, political agitation focussed on repealing it, and Franklin now played a key role in England. Although he did not use the snake map again as a propaganda image, Franklin and others made use of related symbolism in other political cartoons. 'MAGNA Britannia, her Colonies REDUC'D', Franklin's third political cartoon, produced in the winter of 1765–6, is also an emblematic picture. Britannia's severed limbs are labelled in geographical order (New Eng[land], New York, Pennsyl[vania] and Virg[inia]), echoing the dissected map. A lance is aimed from New England at the breast of Britannia. Her representation as a classical figure and the banner referring to Bellisarius, a once-famous Roman general impoverished and imprisoned by the jealous Emperor, also contribute to the symbolism.[67]

Rather than publish this political cartoon, Franklin circulated it privately. A fashion in late eighteenth-century London was the printing of political cartoons on small pasteboard cards for distribution or binding into booklets. Amateurs like Franklin, as

*Fig. 4.* 'The Curious Zebra', 1783. British Museum, Dept. of Prints and Drawings, BM. 5487. *By courtesy of the Trustees of the British Museum*

well as leading artists of the day, made sketches and had them engraved and printed. Mary Darly, the wife of the main publisher of political cards, wrote a guide to the drawing of caricatures.[68] Franklin sent his 'MAGNA Britannia' cards to friends, used them as note paper 'to write all his Messages to Men in power in Great Britain', 'employed a Waiter to place one of them in each Parliament Mans hand as he entred the house the day preceding the great debate of the Stamp Act', and even left them as his final visiting cards before his departure from England at the start of the American Revolution in 1775.[69]

Among other British political cartoons inspired by the Stamp Act is the snake cartoon's most exotic relative, 'THE CURIOUS ZEBRA. alive from America!' (fig. 4). The zebra's stripes are labelled in geographical order with the names of the thirteen American colonies. Various political figures look on, while George Grenville attempts to place on its back a saddle labelled 'Stamp Act'.[70]

'The TEA-TAX-TEMPEST, or OLD TIME with his MAGICK=LANTHERN',

101

another British political cartoon published in 1783 at the close of the Revolutionary War, takes a retrospective look at the beginnings of rebellion during the Stamp Act crisis. In this cartoon, Father Time projects a magic-lantern medley of images before an audience which includes personifications of Britannia and America (the latter as an Indian maiden). Issuing from an exploding teapot is the undulating snake of the cartoon; a similar snake is stretched across the striped ground of a flag. The explanatory text reads, 'There you see the little Hot Spit Fire Tea pot that has done all the Mischief... There you see the thirteen Stripes and Rattle = Snake exalted... &c. &c. &c.'.[71] The magic-lantern theme recalls the practice of displaying oil-paper transparencies of patriotic scenes and symbols in windows or at evening meetings. The Boston silversmith and revolutionary, Paul Revere, had fashioned such affecting transparencies that it was reported that 'spectators were struck with solemn silence and their countenances were covered with a melancholy gloom'.[72] One such patriotic symbol was the snake from Franklin's cartoon, which also inspired a number of flag designs during the Revolutionary War period.[73]

The snake cartoon made one more appearance between the Stamp Act crisis in 1765 and the American Revolution. When the hated Governor of Massachusetts, Sir Francis Bernard, returned to England in 1769, he was saluted with a volley of derogatory newspaper articles and poems. The snake map appeared on the verso of a poem printed in Boston, titled 'An Elegy to the infamous Memory of Sr. F—— B——'. The print is identical with the Boston version of the snake map which appeared in *The Constitutional Courant* of 1765. Beneath the snake image are four lines of verse adapting the symbolism to the occasion:

> Not the harsh Threats of Tyrants bearing Rule,
> Nor Guile-cloak'd-Meekness of each cringing Tool;
> Shall shake our Firmness, or divide That Love
> Which the strong Ties of social Friendship prove.[74]

### AMERICAN REVOLUTIONARY WAR

During the American Revolution, however, the snake map would reappear in a more general context. By 1775 there were almost forty newspapers in the American colonies, and a paper war raged on their pages at the same time that battles were being fought on the ground.[75] The snake map appeared as a masthead design in three of those papers, continuing the precedent set by *The Constitutional Courant*. On 23 June 1774 John Holt, the publisher of *The New-York Journal*, changed the masthead design from the traditional British Royal Arms to a new version of the snake map, thus advertising the paper's revolutionary sympathies. In Holt's version the snake is divided into nine parts with 'G' for Georgia added at the tail; it has lost its loop; and the motto is now 'UNITE OR DIE'. By 27 July 1774 it had been copied in the masthead of *The Pennsylvania Journal* published by William and Thomas Bradford. The only notable difference is that the Georgia tail portion of the Pennsylvania version is divided into two segments. *The*

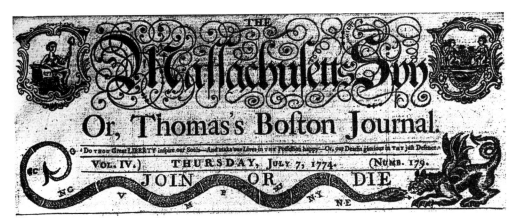

*Fig. 5.* The snake-and-dragon masthead from *The Massachusetts Spy*, 7 July 1774. From A. Matthews, *The Snake Devices*, 1908. BL, 011902.f.84

*New-York Journal* used the snake map as a masthead until 8 December 1774, while *The Pennsylvania Journal* used it until 18 October 1775.[76]

At the same time a more innovative variation of the snake map showed up in the masthead of a Boston paper, *The Massachusetts Spy* (fig. 5). The publisher, Isaiah Thomas, later wrote that:

On the 7th of July, 1774, ... a new political device appeared in the title of this paper — a snake and a dragon. The dragon represented Greatbritain, and the snake the colonies. The snake was divided into nine parts, the head was one part, and under it N.E. as representing Newengland; the second part N.Y. for Newyork; the third N.J. for Newjersey; the fourth P. for Pennsylvania; the fifth M. for Maryland; the sixth V. for Virginia; the seventh N.C. for Northcarolina; the eighth S.C. for Southcarolina; and the ninth part, or tail, for Georgia. The head and tail of the snake were supplied with stings, for defence against the dragon, which appeared furious, and as bent on attacking the snake. Over several parts of the snake, was this motto, in large capitals, 'JOIN OR DIE!' This device, which was extended under the whole width of the title of the *Spy*, appeared in every succeeding paper whilst it was printed in Boston.[77]

The American snake confronting the British dragon gives dramatic visual emphasis to the line of text just below the newspaper title: 'Do THOU Great LIBERTY inspire our Souls — And make our Lives in THY Possession happy — Or, our Deaths glorious in THY just Defence.' The last appearance of *The Massachusetts Spy* in Boston, and hence of the snake-and-dragon design, was 6 April 1775.[78]

The design of the snake appearing in the three newspaper mastheads during 1774–5 has been generalized, and its curves no longer suggest the coastline. This is particularly true of *The Massachusetts Spy* where the snake has been elongated across the page. However, the maplike geographical sequence of the colonies remains. *The Massachusetts Spy* masthead is of particular interest, because it was executed by Paul Revere, the

Boston silversmith famous for his midnight ride in 1775 to warn of approaching British troops. Revere's revolutionary sentiments were also expressed in his printed engravings and metalcuts. His surviving day books record not only his work in silver but also, with a versatility typical of the period, many commissions to engrave maps, music, advertising cards, currency, portraits, caricatures, and the like for intaglio or relief printing.[79] For example, after the Boston Massacre in 1770 Revere produced a copper engraving of the event and also, for *The Boston Gazette*, a metalcut showing the coffins of the patriots slain by the British soldiers. He had provided the scrollwork title for *The Massachusetts Spy* in 1771, and on 6 July 1774 he charged the publisher twelve shillings for cutting the accompanying snake-and-dragon design. He often adapted designs from existing pictorial models. The likely inspiration for the snake-and-dragon design was Revere's own intaglio satirical print, 'A View of the Year 1765', itself an adaptation of a British print of 1763. The original print had depicted opposition in Britain to the Excise Bill of 1763, the latter personified as a dragon. Revere's version in 1765 modified the dragon to represent the Stamp Act and showed his opponents as a row of figures, eight of whom (labelled by initials) represent the American colonies. For *The Massachusetts Spy* masthead Revere updated and simplified the imagery to suit the metalcut medium, replacing the figures by the American snake facing the British dragon.[80]

The snake cartoon appeared frequently on newspaper mastheads in New York, Boston and Philadelphia during 1774–5. Instead of responding in kind, the Royalist press replied poetically. *The New-York Gazetteer* opened the lively exchange of verse on 25 August 1774 with the following lines:

For the NEW-YORK GAZETTEER.
On the SNAKE, depicted at the Head of some American NEWS PAPERS.

Ye Sons of Sedition, how comes it to pass,
That America's typed by a SNAKE — in the grass?
Don't you think 'tis a scandalous, saucy reflection,
That merits the soundest, severest Correction,
NEW-ENGLAND's the Head too; — NEW ENGLAND's abused;
For the Head of the Serpent we know *should* be Bruised.[81]

Rejoinders appeared in *The Pennsylvania Journal* on 31 August, *The Massachusetts Spy* and *The New-York Journal* on 15 September. A further reply whose opening lines echo the cartographic imagery of the snake map appeared in *The New-York Journal* on 29 September and was reprinted in *The Massachusetts Spy* on 27 October:

*On the* BRITISH MINISTRY, *and* New-England, *the* Head *of the* AMERICAN SNAKE.
AN EPIGRAM. 1774.

Britain's sons line the coasts of Atlantic all o'er,
Great of length, but in breadth they *now* wind on a shore
That's divided by inlets, by creeks, and by bays, —
A snake* cut in parts, a pat emblem convey —

The *fell junto* at home — sure their heads are but froth —
Fain this snake would have caught to supply *viper broth*
For their *worn* constitution — and to it they go,
Hurry *Tom*, without his yes or his no,
On the boldest adventure *their* annals can show:
By their *wisdom* advised, he *their courage* displays,
For they seiz'd on the *tongue* 'mong their first of essays;
Nor once thought of the *teeth*, when *our* snake they assail —
Tho' the prudent catch snakes by the back or the tail —
To direct to the head! — our GOOD KING *must* indite 'em —
They forgot that the *head* would most certainly bite 'em.

*Some fifty years hence, when the body fills up, an elephant supporting Great Britain on his back, will be a more proper emblem.[82]

No longer a novelty, the snake cartoon had become a political icon.

During the course of the Revolutionary War the snake design was further modified, shedding its cartographic aspect to emphasize the theme of unity. When John Holt, the publisher of *The New-York Journal*, stopped using the snake map in the masthead, he immediately replaced it on 15 December 1774 with a circular snake design which appeared until 29 August 1776. A contemporary description reads:

The snake was united, and coiled with the tail in its mouth, forming a double ring; within the ring was a pillar standing on Magna Charta, and surmounted with the cap of liberty; the pillar on each side was supported by six arms and hands, figurative of the colonies.[83]

The inscription on the body of the snake reinforces this imagery:

UNITED NOW ALIVE AND FREE – FIRM ON THIS BASIS LIBERTY SHALL STAND * AND THUS SUPPORTED EVER BLESS OUR LAND * TILL TIME BECOMES ETERNITY.[84]

The circular snake as the symbol of eternity was, of course, a familiar emblematic image, but other American snake symbolism was also developing.

A letter published in *The Pennsylvania Journal* and also in *The Pennsylvania Gazette* in 1775 extols the rattlesnake as a suitable American symbol, because it is vigilant, only attacks in self-defence, never surrenders and its thirteen rattles symbolize the union of the thirteen American colonies:

'Tis curious and amazing to observe how distinct and independent of each other the rattles of this animal are, and yet how firmly they are united together so as to be never separated except by breaking them to pieces. One of these rattles is incapable of producing a sound; but the ringing of thirteen together is sufficient to alarm the boldest man living.[85]

The acceptance of the rattlesnake as an American emblem is also shown by its appearance on paper currency, uniform buttons, and naval and military flags.[86]

In its new role as a national symbol the snake image was once again linked with

Benjamin Franklin. Based in France from 1776 to 1785, Franklin fought with words and diplomacy on America's behalf and became a legendary figure in old age. Among the many portraits painted of him during his stay in France was one by Joseph-Siffred Duplessis, who first exhibited it at the Salon of 1779 and later made numerous copies of the subject. The original version is mounted in an elaborate gilded frame ornamented with carvings symbolic of Franklin's role in the struggle for American independence: a liberty cap, a liberty torch, a flayed lion skin and a rattlesnake.[87] Interpreted generally, the snake could represent wisdom or prudence, but its undulating shape and single coil are unmistakably those of Franklin's original snake map of 1754. Here is the once-divided snake which has united to defeat the British lion, represented by its flayed skin. When the leading London cartoonist of that day, James Gillray, published a print showing the American rattlesnake encircling the defeated British troops at Yorktown in 1782,[88] it must have seemed that the life history of the snake map had drawn to a fitting close.

## AMERICAN CIVIL WAR

However, there is an epilogue to the tale of the snake map. In 1861, as the Civil War threatened to split the United States over the issue of slavery, both the northern Unionists and the southern Secessionists employed graphic propaganda. The political cartoon, by now a traditional means of attack and repartee, appeared separately and in newspapers and magazines.

One such cartoon titled 'Scott's Great Snake' was published in Cincinnati by J. B. Elliott in 1866 (fig. 6). It illustrates the proposal, popularly dubbed the 'Anaconda Plan', of the aged but cunning General-in-Chief, Winfield Scott, to strangle the insurrection by

... a complete blockade of the Atlantic and Gulf ports soon to commence. In connection with such a blockade, we propose a powerful move down the Mississippi to the ocean, with a cordon of ports at proper points ... the object being to clear out and keep open this great line of communication in connection with the strict blockade of the seaboard, so as to envelop the insurgent States and bring them to terms with less bloodshed than by any other plan.[89]

The cartoon shows a snake patterned with the stars and stripes of the American flag encircling the Confederate States. Reminiscent of Gillray's copper engraving of the American rattlesnake encircling the British at Yorktown a century earlier, but less refined in style, this nineteenth-century lithograph compensates for its crudity by the energetic portrayal of the snake and the malicious fun of its humorous details. In any event, hotter heads prevailed, and the Union side adopted instead General George McClellan's plan 'to subdue the seceded states by piece meal', a course of action which resulted in victory, but only after the long, bloody conflict that General Scott had predicted.[90]

During the mid-nineteenth century a new method of circulating political propaganda came into use. Following the earlier British example, a change in American postal

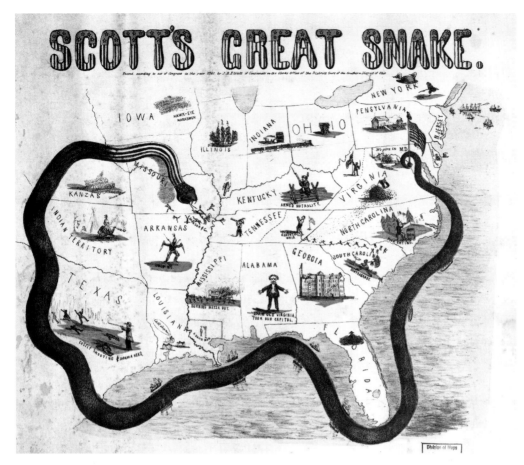

*Fig. 6.* 'Scott's Great Snake'. *By courtesy of the Library of Congress Geography and Map Division*

regulations in 1845 meant that envelopes no longer incurred an additional charge. Thus encouraged, the American envelope industry developed rapidly.[91] An innovation copied from England and taken taken up by the protagonists in the American Civil War was to print a patriotic image, either straightforward or satirical, on the envelope.[92] Clearly drawing upon the emblem tradition, such designs often included a motto and short explanatory text, as well as a graphic image. Southerners found a design source for such patriotic covers in the imagery of the American Revolution, which they consciously revived to rally public opinion to their cause. The Secessionists felt that they, like the American colonies during the Revolutionary War, were rebelling against an oppressive central government. In addition to envelopes used during the Civil War, other unused ones with fictitious imprints appear to have been produced later as souvenirs.[93]

One such envelope design incorporates a new version of the snake cartoon with the

The device of our Fathers in their first struggle for liberty, —1776.

UNITE OR DIE

"SLAVE STATES, once more let me repeat, that the only way of preserving our slave property, or what we prize more than life, our LIBERTY, is by a UNION WITH EACH OTHER."

*Jefferson Davis.*

G W Falen, Printer, 216 King St. near Market Charleston S C C S A.

*Fig. 7.* Confederate Decorative Cover. *By courtesy of the Florida Federation of Stamp Clubs*

printer's name given as G. W. Falen of Charleston, South Carolina (fig. 7). No postally used example is known, and a search of historical records in Charleston has failed to trace a printer named G. W. Falen, so this may have been a post-war souvenir envelope.[94] The allusion to the American Revolution is made clear by a line of text at the top: 'The device of our Fathers in their first struggle for liberty, – 1776.' Below this the motto 'UNITE OR DIE' appears in crudely cut letters. The snake, undulating from left to right, is divided into segments labelled with the initials of the fifteen slave-holding states (eleven later joined the Confederacy). The names are not in geographical order, so the map symbolism has been lost. However, the symbolic imagery of the snake has been supplemented by a palmetto tree which serves as a mast for a seven-star Confederate flag of the 'stars and bars' type. The device of the South Carolina seal and flag, a palmetto tree with a rattlesnake coiled about the base, has supplied the additional symbolism.[95] Beneath the snake is printed a statement by Jefferson Davis, the President of the Southern Confederacy: 'SLAVE STATES, once more let me repeat, that the only way of preserving our slave property, or what we prize more than life, our LIBERTY, is by a UNION WITH EACH OTHER.'

Whether Benjamin Franklin would have agreed or disagreed with the sentiments expressed is not at issue here. However, remembering his timely circulation of political cartoons by means of pamphlets, newspapers and political cards, one has to conclude that the prompt exploitation of new propagandizing media, such as the envelope, would have suited the Franklin style of operation.

By the time the snake cartoon was revived during the American Civil War, the mixture of map, snake and dismemberment symbolism had almost lost its potency. My own rough tally of Confederate and Union patriotic covers identified numerous map images (mostly conventional location maps and bird's-eye views), several dozen snake motifs and a few with dissection imagery (e.g. a segmented arch representing the Union, each stone bearing the name of a state), but no cover which combines all three symbolic strands.[96] The segmented snake on the Confederate envelope (fig. 7) is no longer a map, while General Scott's snake (fig. 6) has lost its segments and metamorphosed into a boa constrictor. After the Union victory which resulted in the preservation of the United States of America, no political context in which the snake cartoon would be relevant has recurred. Considering that the snake cartoon may now have come to the end of its symbolic life, it deserves a brief epitaph.

In his political writings, Franklin characteristically used the medium of print to inform and persuade, making the serious message more palatable and memorable with a touch of humour. He also used the graphic image as visual propaganda to enhance the emotive power of the printed word. Combining various symbolic themes, including that of the map, his snake cartoon was meant to convey a particular message for an immediate purpose. However, released into the sphere of public knowledge, the snake image took on an independent existence in the popular imagination. Its evolutionary cycle of intermittent rebirth continued as long as the symbolic combination remained viable. Like Peter Pan, though, the snake cartoon could live in men's minds only as long as they believed in it. Considered by itself, the snake cartoon permits no further generalizations. As an example of a genre, however, its life story enhances our understanding of cartographic imagery in the broader history of graphic symbolism.

Thanks for assistance with research for this paper are due to David Beech of the British Library Philatelic Collections, John R. Brumgardt and Mary Giles of the Charleston Museum, Ralph Ehrenberg and Ronald Grim of the Library of Congress Geography and Map Division, and Pamela Scott of Cornell University.

1 In 'The Snake Devices, 1754–1776 and the Constitutional Courant, 1765', *Publications of the Colonial Society of Massachusetts*, xi (1906–7), pp. 409–52 (reprinted Cambridge, 1908), Albert Matthews dissects the earlier 'mainly inaccurate' literature on the snake cartoon in a bibliographical study which remains authoritative, even though more recent writers like Frank H. Sommer, 'Emblem and Device: the Origin of the Great Seal of the United States', *The Art Quarterly*, xxiv (1961), pp. 63–4 and Wm. R. Furlong and B. McCandless, *So Proudly We Hail: the History of the United States Flag* (Washington, D.C., 1981), pp. 521, 71–77, have introduced iconographical aspects of snake imagery largely untouched by Matthews.

2 A. Johnson and D. Malone (eds.), *Dictionary of American Biography* (London, 1931), vol. vi, p. 589.

3 Leonard W. Labaree *et al.* (eds.), *The Papers of Benjamin Franklin* [Franklin, *Papers*] (New Haven and London, 1959–), vol. v, pp. 160, 269–80, 335–8; Max Farrand (ed.), *Benjamin Franklin's Memoirs* [Franklin, *Memoirs*] (Berkeley and Los Angeles, 1949), pp. 324–9.

4 Franklin, *Papers*, vol. v, pp. 274–5.

5 Franklin, *Memoirs*, pp. 278–9.

6 William Murrell, *A History of American Graphic Humor* (New York, 1933), vol. i, p. 11.

7 William C. Miller, 'Benjamin Franklin's Philadelphia Printing 1728–1766: a Descriptive Bibliography', *Memoirs of the American Philosophical Society*, cii (1974), pp. 219–20.

8 Franklin, *Papers*, vol. v, pp. 272–3.

9 Edwin Wolf, 2nd, 'Benjamin Franklin's Stamp

Act Cartoon', *Proceedings of the American Philosophical Society*, xcix (1955), p. 388.

10 Arthur M. Schlesinger, *Prelude to Independence: the Newspaper War on Britain 1764–1776* (New York, 1958), p. 45.

11 Franklin, *Memoirs*, pp. 280–1.

12 Franklin, *Papers*, vol. xxii, pp. 357–8.

13 Sinclair Hamilton, *Early American Book Illustrators and Wood Engravers 1670–1870* (Princeton, 1958), p. xxv.

14 Franklin, *Memoirs*, pp. 136–9.

15 Ibid., pp. 142–3.

16 James Clements Wheat and Christian F. Brun, *Maps and Charts Published in America before 1800: a Bibliography* (New Haven and London, 1969), p. 102.

17 Hamilton, pp. xxvi, 8; Miller, p. 215.

18 Martha Gandy Fales, 'Heraldic and Emblematic Engravers of Colonial Boston', in *Boston Prints and Printmakers 1670–1775. A Conference held by the Colonial Society of Massachusetts, 1 and 2 April 1971* (Boston, 1973), p. 218; L. H. Gipson, *Lewis Evans* (Philadelphia, 1939), p. 7.

19 Andreas Alciatus, *D. And. Alciati Emblemata* (Lyons, 1564), p. 144.

20 Rosemary Freeman, *English Emblem Books* (1948; reprinted New York, 1978), pp. 1–35.

21 Dorothy M. George, *English Political Caricature to 1792: a Study of Opinion and Propaganda* (Oxford, 1959), pp. 3–43.

22 Freeman, p. 210.

23 Franklin, *Memoirs*, pp. 30–3, 108–11, 128–9.

24 Franklin, *Papers*, vol. xv, p. 300.

25 Sommer, p. 62.

26 Edwin Wolf, 2nd, 'Introduction', in *A Catalogue of Books belonging to the Library Company of Philadelphia. A Facsimile of the Edition of 1741 Printed by Benjamin Franklin* (Philadelphia, 1956), pp. iii–v.

27 Edwin Wolf, 2nd, 'The Reconstruction of Benjamin Franklin's Library: an Unorthodox Jigsaw Puzzle', *Papers of the Bibliographical Society of America*, lvi (1962), pp. 1–16.

28 Franklin, *Papers*, vol. v, pp. 272–3.

29 Wolf, 'Benjamin Franklin's Stamp Act Cartoon', p. 388.

30 Ibid., p. 391.

31 Ibid., p. 390.

32 Franklin, *Papers*, vol. ii, p. 237.

33 Ibid., vols. v, p. 330; xii, p. 423.

34 Nicholas Hans, 'Franklin, Jefferson and the English Radicals at the End of the Eighteenth Century', *Proceedings of the American Philosophical Society*, xcviii (1954), p. 421.

35 Franklin, *Papers*, vol. xiii, p. 214.

36 Gipson, pp. 3, 6, 9, 78.

37 *History of the U.S. Postal Service 1775–1980*, U.S. Postal Service Publication 100 (Washington, D.C., 1981), p. 1.

38 Louis De Vorsey, 'Pioneer Charting of the Gulf Stream: the Contributions of Benjamin Franklin and William Gerard De Brahm', *Imago Mundi*, xxviii (1976), pp. 105–11; Philip L. Richardson, 'Benjamin Franklin and Timothy Folger's First Printed Chart of the Gulf Stream', *Science*, ccvii (1980), pp. 643–4.

39 Franklin, *Papers*, vol. v, pp. 274, 457–8.

40 George, pp. 26–8.

41 Michael Drayton, *Poly-Olbion* (London, 1613). See J. B. Harley, 'Meaning and Ambiguity in Tudor Cartography', in Sarah Tyacke (ed.), *English Map-Making 1500–1650* (London, 1983), p. 39, pl. 15.

42 George, p. 62.

43 Freeman, p. 22.

44 Angus K. Gillespie and Jay Mechling, *American Wildlife in Symbol and Story* (Knoxville, 1987), pp. 5–6.

45 Lawrence Monroe Klauber, *Rattlesnakes: their Habits, Life Histories, and Influence on Mankind* (Berkeley & Los Angeles, 1956), p. 351.

46 George, pp. 48, 60, 101–2.

47 Klauber, p. 350.

48 Nicolas Verrien, *Livre curieux et utile pour les sçavans et artistes* (Paris, 1685?). This emblem is discussed by Pamela Scott in '"Temple of Liberty": Building a Capitol for a New Nation', *Library of Congress Information Bulletin*, liv, no. 6 (1995), p. 118, and by Sommer, p. 63.

49 Mark Catesby, *The Natural History of Carolina, Florida and the Bahama Islands* (London, 1731–48), vol. ii, p. 41.

50 *The Pennsylvania Gazette*, 9 May 1751, as quoted in Franklin, *Papers*, vol. iv, pp. 131–3.

51 Catesby, vol. ii, p. 59, plates 41, 42, 52, 53.

52 George, pp. 49, 118, 132.

53 Franklin, *Papers*, vol. xiii, pp. 66–72.

54 Franklin, *Memoirs*, pp. 350–1.

55 Stephen Hess and Milton Kaplan, *The Ungentlemanly Art: a History of American Political Cartoons* (New York, 1975), p. 58.

56 Michael Warner, *The Letters of the Republic:*

*Publication and the Public Sphere in Eighteenth-Century America* (Cambridge, Mass., 1990), pp. 30, 65–6, 68.

57 Franklin, *Papers*, vol. xiv, p. 345.

58 Matthews, pp. 417–18.

59 Franklin, *Memoirs*, p. 326.

60 Keith Williams, *The English Newspaper: an Illustrated History to 1900* (London, 1977), pp. 24–5.

61 Warner, pp. 68–71.

62 Franklin, *Papers*, vol. xii, pp. 287–8; Matthews, pp. 421–46.

63 Edmund S. Morgan and Helen M. Morgan, *The Stamp Act Crisis: Prologue to Revolution* (Chapel Hill, 1953), p. 103.

64 Ibid., pp. 105–7.

65 Matthews, p. 436.

66 Leslie Stephen and Sidney Lee (eds.), *Dictionary of National Biography* [*D.N.B.*] (London, 1908), vol. iv, pp. 716–17.

67 Franklin, *Papers*, vol. xiii, pp. 66–7; George, pp. 136–7.

68 George, pp. 115–18, 128–9, 134.

69 Franklin, *Papers*, vol. xiii, p. 69; Wolf, 'Benjamin Franklin's Stamp Act Cartoon', pp. 389–90.

70 George, p. 156, pl. 50.

71 *The American War of Independence 1775–83. A Commemorative Exhibition Organized by the Map Library and the Department of Manuscripts of the British Library Reference Division 4 July to 11 November 1975* (London, 1975), p. 160, no. 183.

72 Schlesinger, p. 43.

73 Geo. Henry Preble, *Our Flag. Origin and Progress of the Flag of the United States of America* (Albany, 1872), pp. 159–67; Edward W. Richardson, *Standards and Colors of the American Revolution* (Philadelphia, 1982), pp. 13–15; Francis Newton Thorpe, *A History of the American People* (Chicago, 1901), p. 116.

74 *D.N.B.*, vol. ii, pp. 380–1.

75 Warner, pp. 65–6.

76 Matthews, pp. 446–8.

77 Ibid., p. 447; I. Thomas, *The History of Printing in America* (Worcester, Mass., 1810), vol. ii, p. 307.

78 Matthews, p. 447, pl. ix.

79 Clarence S. Brigham, *Paul Revere's Engravings* (New York, 1969), pp. 3–6.

80 Ibid., pp. 52–78, 199–202, 209; Hess and Kaplan, pp. 54–7.

81 Matthews, p. 448.

82 Ibid., p. 450.

83 Ibid., p. 447; Thomas, vol. ii, p. 307.

84 Furlong and McCandless, p. 71; Matthews, p. 447.

85 Furlong and McCandless, pp. 71–2; Gillespie and Mechling, p. 53; Preble, pp. 147–50.

86 Furlong and McCandless, pp. 71–4; Willis F. Johnson, *The National Flag: a History* (Boston and New York, 1930), pp. 1, 23–4; Eric P. Newman, *The Early Paper Money of America* (Racine, 1967), p. 314; Milo M. Quaife, Melvin J. Weig and Roy E. Appleman, *The History of the United States Flag from the Revolution to the Present* (New York, 1961), p. 27.

87 Jules Belleudy, *J.-S. Duplessis peintre du roi 1725–1802* (Chartres, 1913), p. 85; Franklin, *Papers*, vol. i, frontispiece, p. xix.

88 Hess and Kaplan, pp. 53, 183.

89 Charles Winslow Elliott, *Winfield Scott: the Soldier and the Man* (New York, 1937), pp. 721–2.

90 Ibid., pp. 722–7.

91 D. Perry Thomas, 'Envelope Beginnings', in *Third American Philatelic Congress. Held under the Auspices of the Chicago Philatelic Society, October 29–30–31, 1937* (Chicago, 1937), pp. 48–9.

92 August Dietz, *The Postal Service of the Confederate States of America* (Richmond, 1929), pp. 346–7.

93 Benjamin Wishnietsky, *Confederate Patriotic Covers and their Uses* (North Miami, 1991), pp. 9, 140.

94 John R. Brumgardt, personal communication, 4 Feb. 1994; George N. Malpass, 'An Interesting Confederate Patriotic Design', *Monthly Bulletin of the Florida Federation of Stamp Clubs* (Mar. 1954), pp. 10–11.

95 Preble, pp. 383–5.

96 The covers surveyed were those illustrated in the comprehensive catalogues by William R. Weiss, *The Catalog of Union Civil War Patriotic Covers* (Bethlehem, Pa., 1995), and Wishnietsky.

# NOTES ON CONTRIBUTORS

KAREN SEVERUD COOK: Curator, Map Library, British Library.

G. MALCOLM LEWIS: 9, Derriman Avenue, Sheffield, S11 9LA; co-editor of Vol. 2.3., *Cartography in the Traditional African, American, Arctic, Australian, and Pacific Societies* (forthcoming), in *The History of Cartography* (University of Chicago Press).

DENNIS REINHARTZ: Professor of History, The University of Texas at Arlington.

KIRSTEN. A. SEAVER: Historian; author of *The Frozen Echo: Greenland and the Exploration of North America, ca. A.D. 1000–1500* (Stanford: Stanford University Press, 1996).

JOAN WINEARLS: Map Librarian, University of Toronto Library.